50 ways to OFF an Elf

This book is the joint intellectual property of James Lincke and Matt Lake. Each brought something to the concept behind the book and to the creation of every page spread. Each of them is slightly in awe of what the other brings to the table, which is how good collaborations should work. Having said that, they did not do this alone. They owe a debt of gratitude to Chris Lake for his skillful and rapid editing of the text, and to all the people who backed this project on Kickstarter, which gave them the funds they needed to bring the project to a conclusion.

Published by Questionable.info

A division of Parnilis Media
of Media, Pennsylvania
www.parnilis.com

ISBN: 069258997X
ISBN-13: 978-0692589977

DEDICATION

Dedication is what you need to stamp out that blight that has contaminated the modern Christmas celebration, the elf.

The elf is indigenous to only three places—the North Pole, Narnia, and Middle Earth. In its natural habitat, the elf maintains steady but healthy population. But after a fashion for adopting elves as exotic pets in all hemispheres of the globe, their population growth has spiraled upwards and out of control.

The Centers for Pest Control have now declared the Elf an invasive hostile species.

They must be stamped out.

This book will help in that endeavor.

Study its methods.

Learn.

And be dedicated.

1. CRUSH WITH CHRISTMAS COOKIES

Ingredients

2 1/4 cups all-purpose flour

1 teaspoon baking soda

Fine salt

1 1/2 sticks (12 tablespoons) unsalted butter, at room temperature

3/4 cup packed light brown sugar

2/3 cup granulated sugar

2 large eggs

1 teaspoon pure vanilla extract

A case of 30 or more 12-ounce bags of semisweet chocolate chips

Instructions

Drop the case of chocolate chip bags on the elf. Remove one 12-ounce bag of chocolate chips and discard the rest as incriminating evidence. Use the one bag of chocolate chips along with the rest of the ingredients to make chocolate chip cookies. Serve the cookies to Santa with the elf concealed beneath the cookies. Pray that Santa has already left your presents by the time he discovers the elf, and that he is too shocked to retrieve them after he discovers the elf.

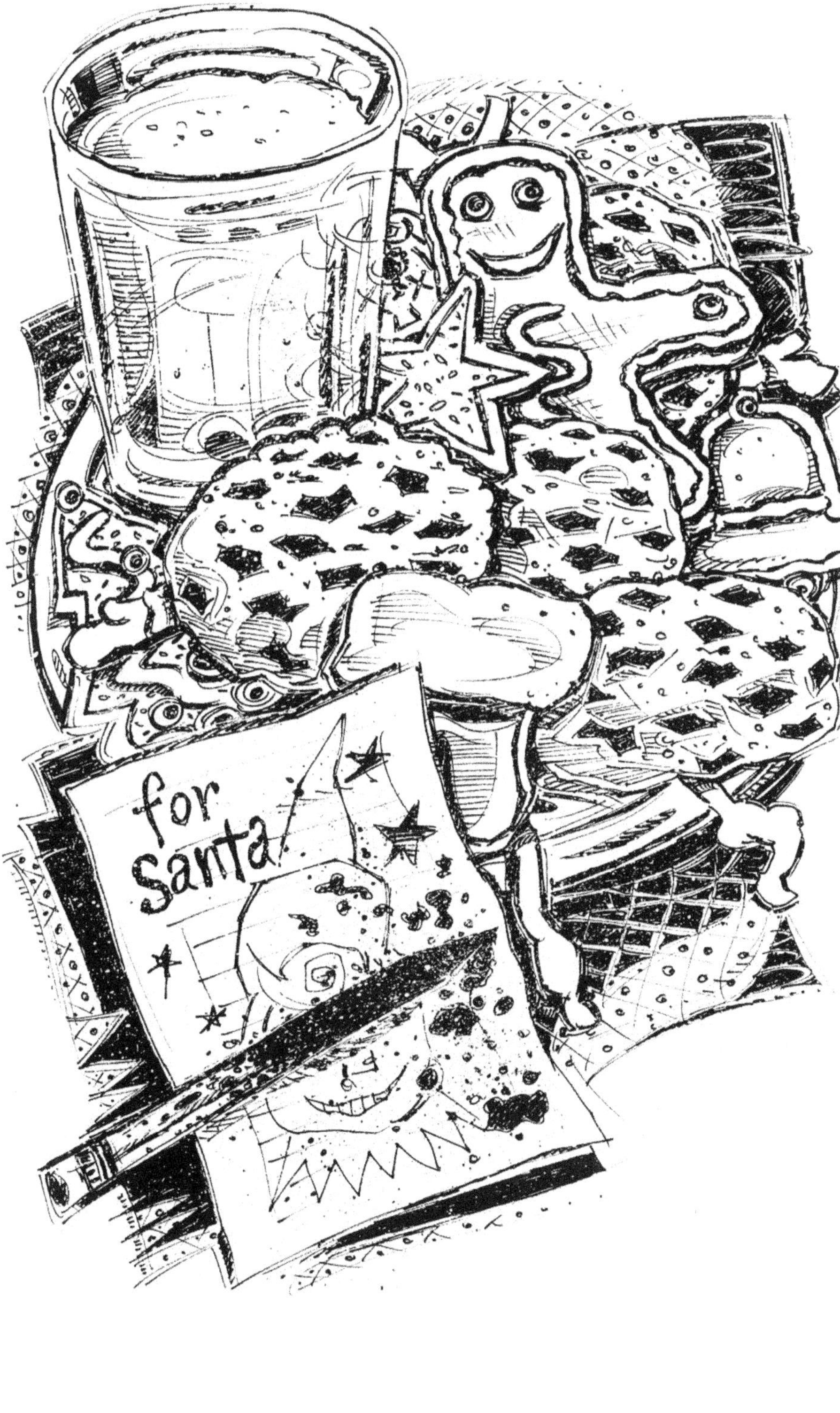
for Santa

2. TAKE HIM ICE FISHING

Plan an ice-fishing trip and invite your elf along. When you arrive at the iced-over lake, take the lump of coal that Santa left for you last Christmas and tie your elf to it. If he protests, explain that it will prevent him from being blown away by any gusts of wind.

Ask the elf to break a hole in the ice using his lump of coal. Shrug at the hapless elf when the coal falls through the fresh ice hole and sinks to the bottom of the lake, dragging the rope, foot, and eventually the whole elf with it.

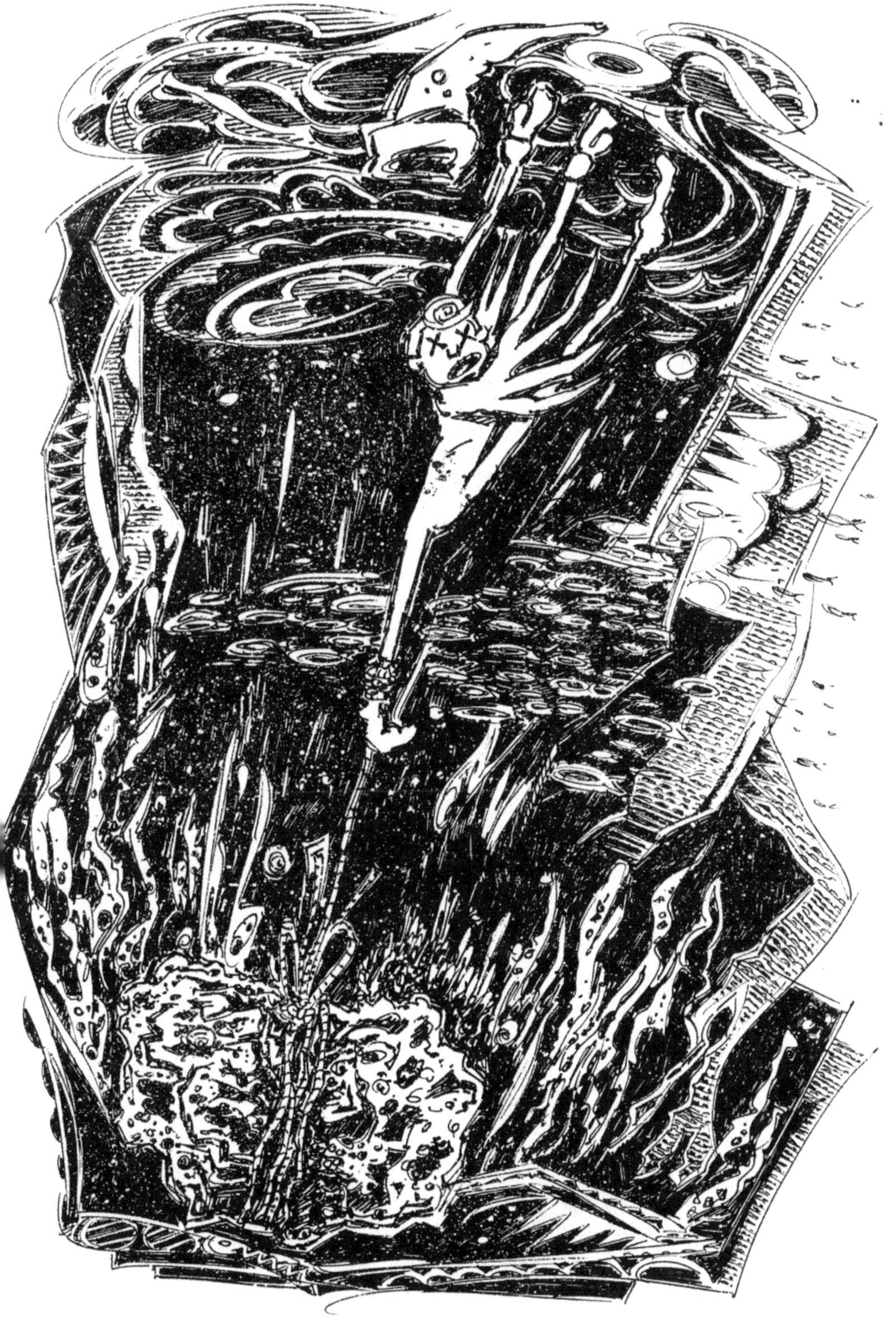

3. TRAMPLED TO DEATH BY THE ROCKETTES

And now, live from the Radio City Music Hall®, we present, as we have every year since 1932, the fabulous Rockettes in our annual Christmas Spectacular. Featuring Ron Hack as Santa Claus, the Rockettes as themselves, and for the first time, introducing our good friend Buddy the Elf as the dance floor.

Take a bow, Buddy.

Buddy?

BUDDY?!?

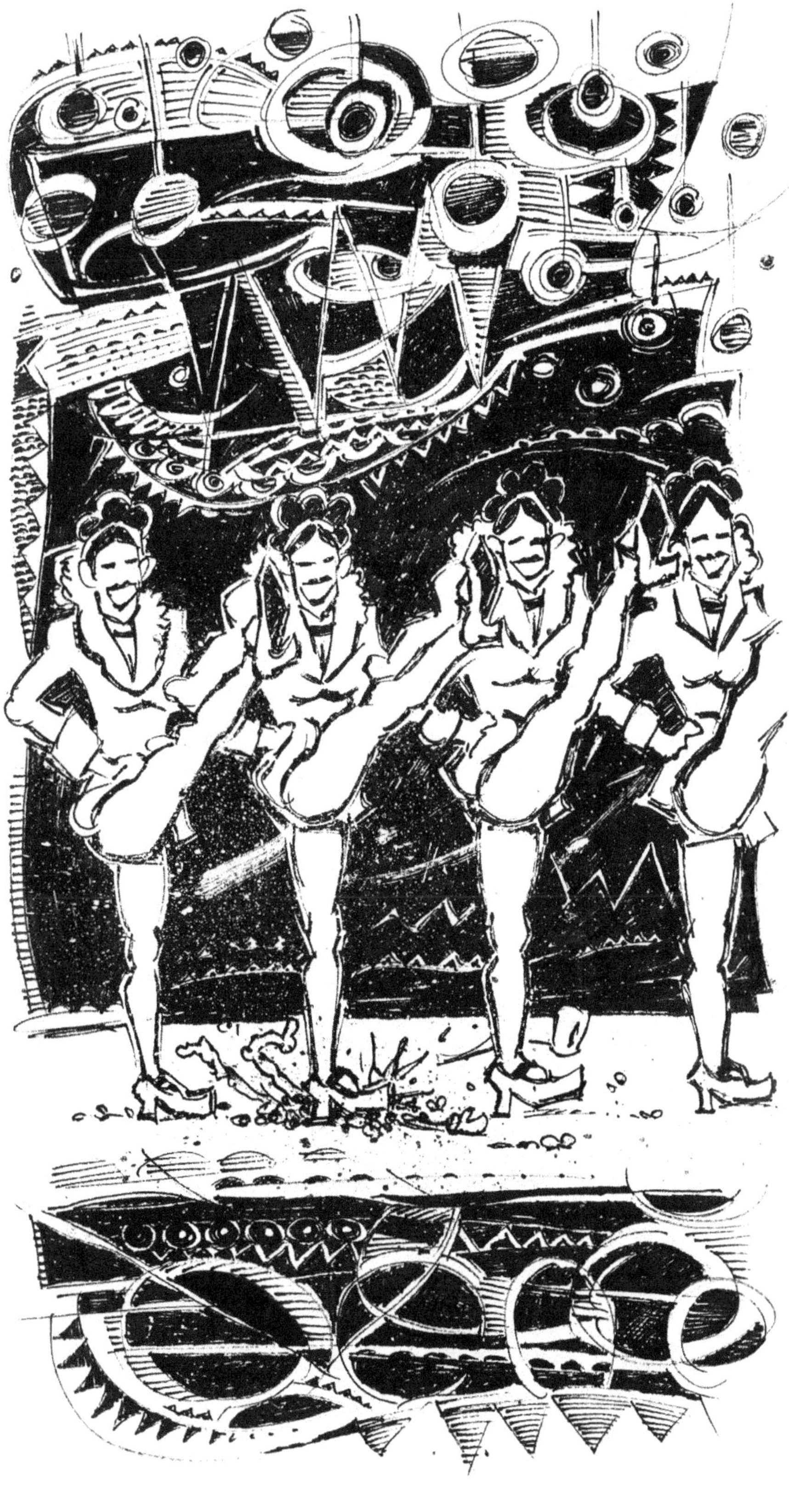

4. DECORATE THE HOUSE WITH AN ELF

Since the late 1950s, competitive house decoration has been a staple of Christmas. The elf is an intensely competitive creature and can easily be motivated to "win Christmas" at the expense of your neighbors. Flatter him, tell him nobody hangs little electric lights from the eaves as well as he does! Look how pretty they are hanging there! What an attractive elf scarf they would make... How nice they look draped around his neck like that...

Then kick away the ladder.

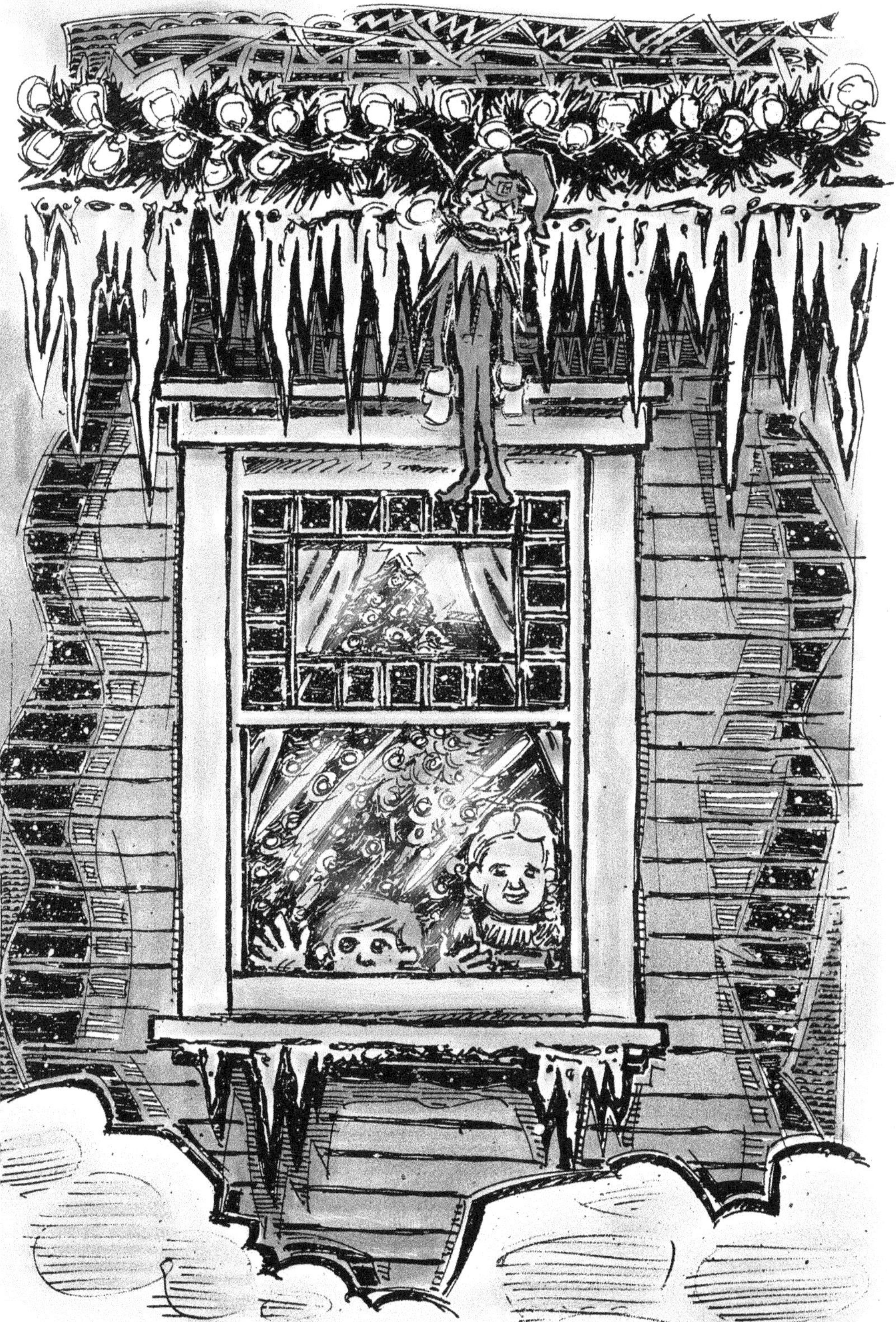

5. PICKING RUDOLPH'S NOSE

They say that you can pick your friends, and you can pick your nose, but you can't pick your friend's nose. This is especially true if your friend is the licensed character Rudolph the Red Nosed Reindeer (© 1939, The Rudolph Company LP, used here for parody purposes only. The view in this picture does not reflect those of the management of Questionable.info, Parnilis Media, or any of its subsidiaries or employees.)

For many years, people assumed that the character Rudolph the Red Nosed Reindeer was just a mutant reindeer with an albino nose—or perhaps a heavy drinker of spiked eggnog. But then Montgomery Ward and The Rudolph Company LP licensed the character to Rankin Bass. The short animated TV movie by Rankin Bass demonstrated that Rudolph's nose was actually a red light bulb powered by dangerous levels of electricity. Or perhaps a robot in reindeer clothing. Either way, the nose can be used as a weapon against elves.

Dare your elf to pick Rudolph's nose. If he seems reluctant, triple dog-dare him. Nobody can back down from a triple dog-dare, so your elf's fate is sealed.

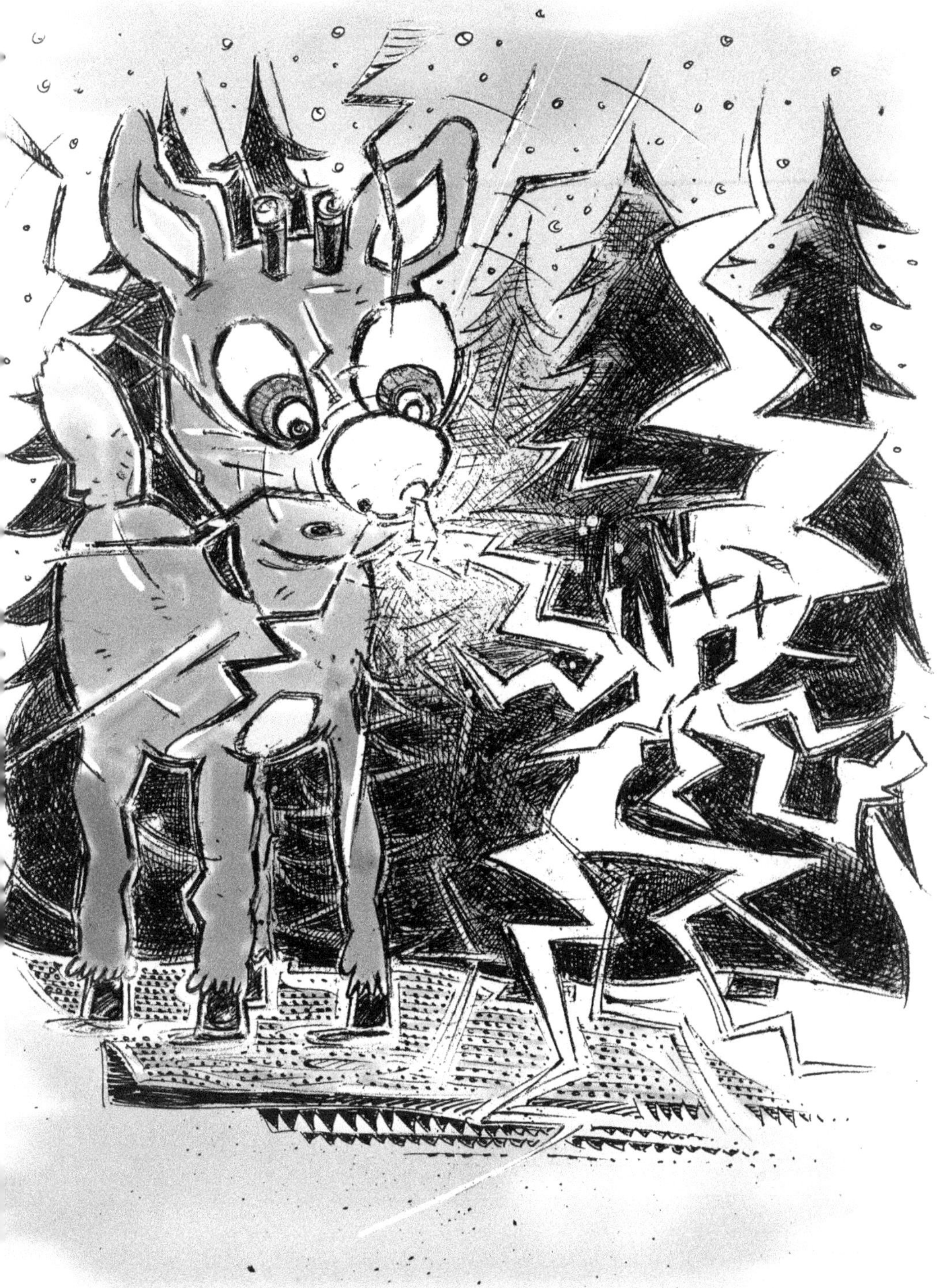

6. PHOTOCOPIED INTO OBLIVION AT THE OFFICE PARTY

The first commercial plain-paper photocopier was the Xerox 914, introduced to the world on September 16, 1959. Part of the reason for its runaway success was that it arrived in corporate offices in time for the holiday party season, where they enabled a new tradition: of sitting on the glass and pressing the copy button.

In a world where folded cards from Hallmark retail at the price of a Starbucks coffee, the butt-copy became an inexpensive alternative greeting received by many close friends of office workers, which propelled the technology responsible even further into the office services market.

Innovations like the selfie-stick have superseded most butt-copy technology in the lucrative holiday-party-greetings market, but traditionalists still favor the photocopier. The mere mention of tradition to an elf is tempting, and as long as you find sufficiently large and drunken employees to follow him onto the photocopier, this method should always yield crushingly good results.

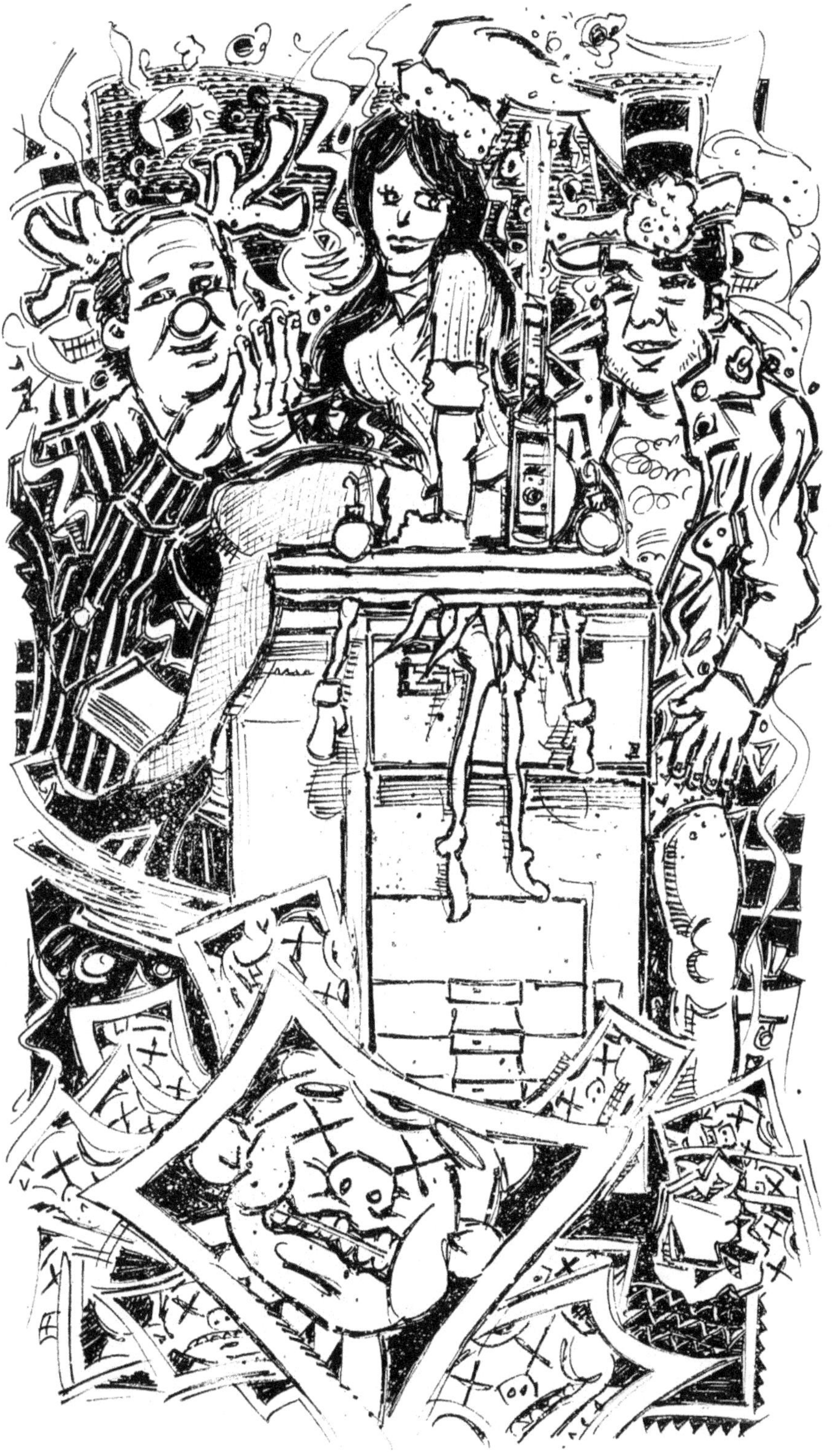

7. SKATED TO BITS AT ROCKEFELLER PLAZA

Looking to break the ice at parties this year? Start with this little tidbit of knowledge: elves as a species are bilaterally symmetrical. And you can prove it with a simple, mirror-base test.

First take your elf to Rockefeller Plaza in the weeks leading up to Christmas. Wait for him to be cut in half by a skate; this should not take long. Then take each half and place it against a mirror. The two half-elf, half-reflection images should look identical, if the elf is indeed bilaterally symmetrical.

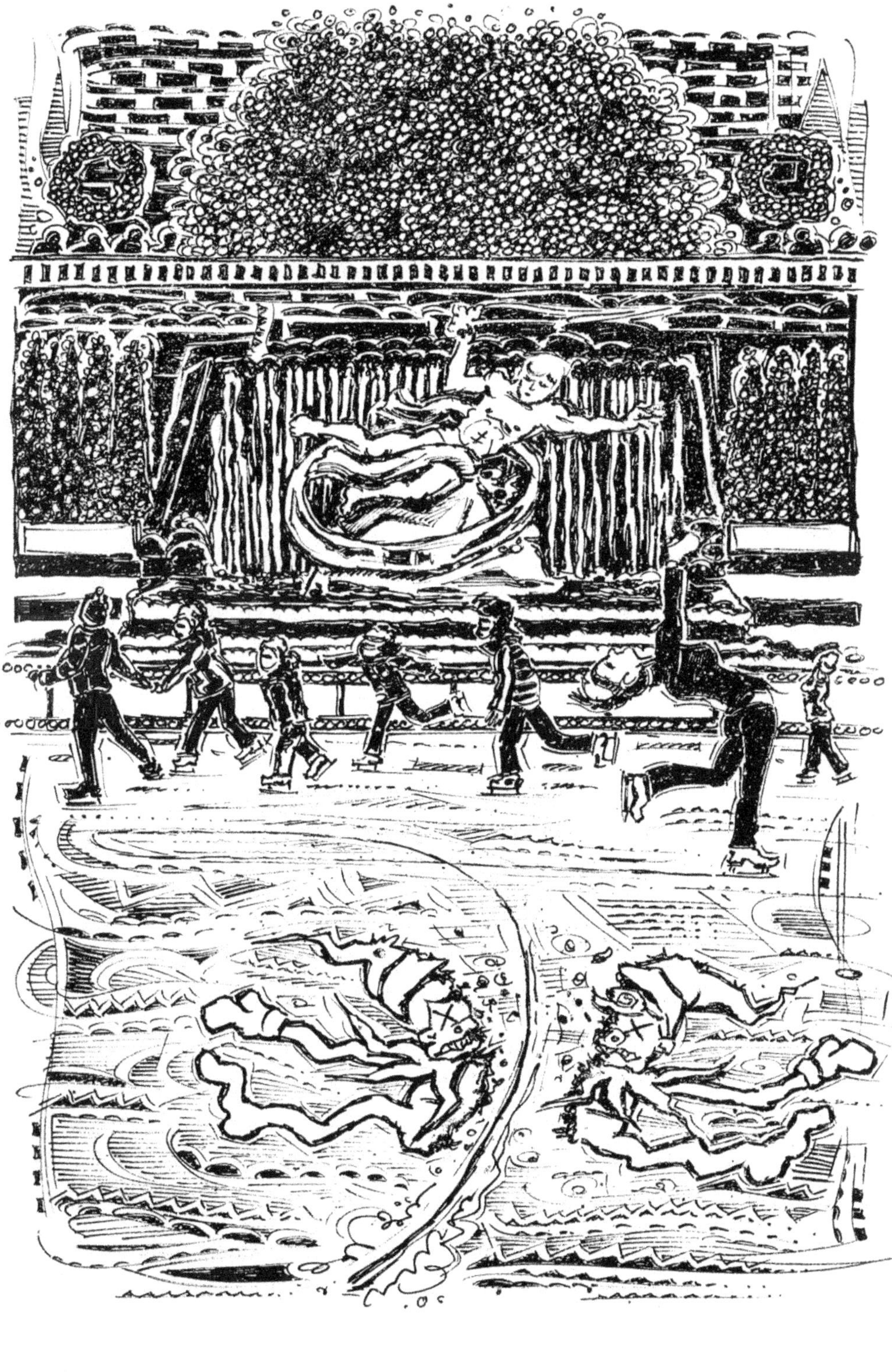

8. PRAY FOR A MIRACLE ON 34TH STREET

Rational thinkers don't believe in miracles. This is because they are unfamiliar with quantum mechanics and the theory of the multiverse.

Multiverse theory holds that there are many, possibly an infinite number, of universes, all existing in parallel. Quantum mechanics holds this truth to be self-evident: Everything that is mathematically possible exists somewhere in some universe.

And so it follows...somewhere in some plane of existence, there is an Elf Street. At some point in some universe, it intersects with 34th Street. And at some fixed point in the time-space continuum, a miracle on 34th Street will lead to a nightmare on Elf Street.

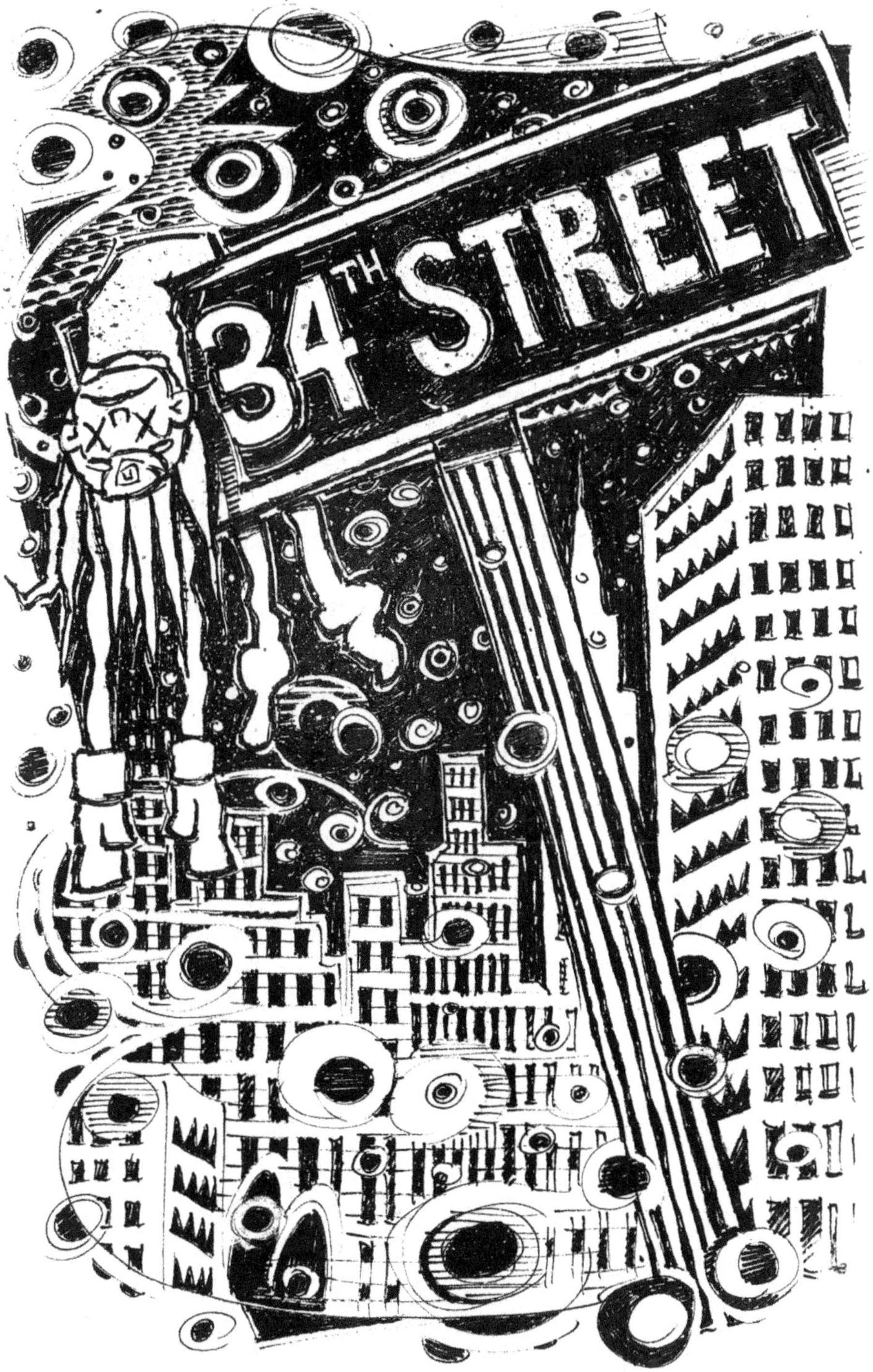
34TH STREET

9. SUI: SLEDDING UNDER THE INFLUENCE

Statistically speaking, intoxicated driving does spike during the holiday season. According to Mothers Against Drunk Driving (MADD), alcohol is a factor in more than half the fatal collisions between Christmas and New Year's Day, which is up ten to twenty percent from the averages year-round. The Centers for Disease Control and Prevention (CDC) estimate that more than 1,200 will die in the United States and more than 25,000 people will be injured in alcohol related injuries.

Now, elves are not smart: quote these statistics to them and they will only hear evidence that everybody's doing it. They'll take a spiked Road 'Nog for the sled home and have a close encounter with a Tannenbaum.

Don't be an elf - don't drink and sled.

You're smarter than an elf.

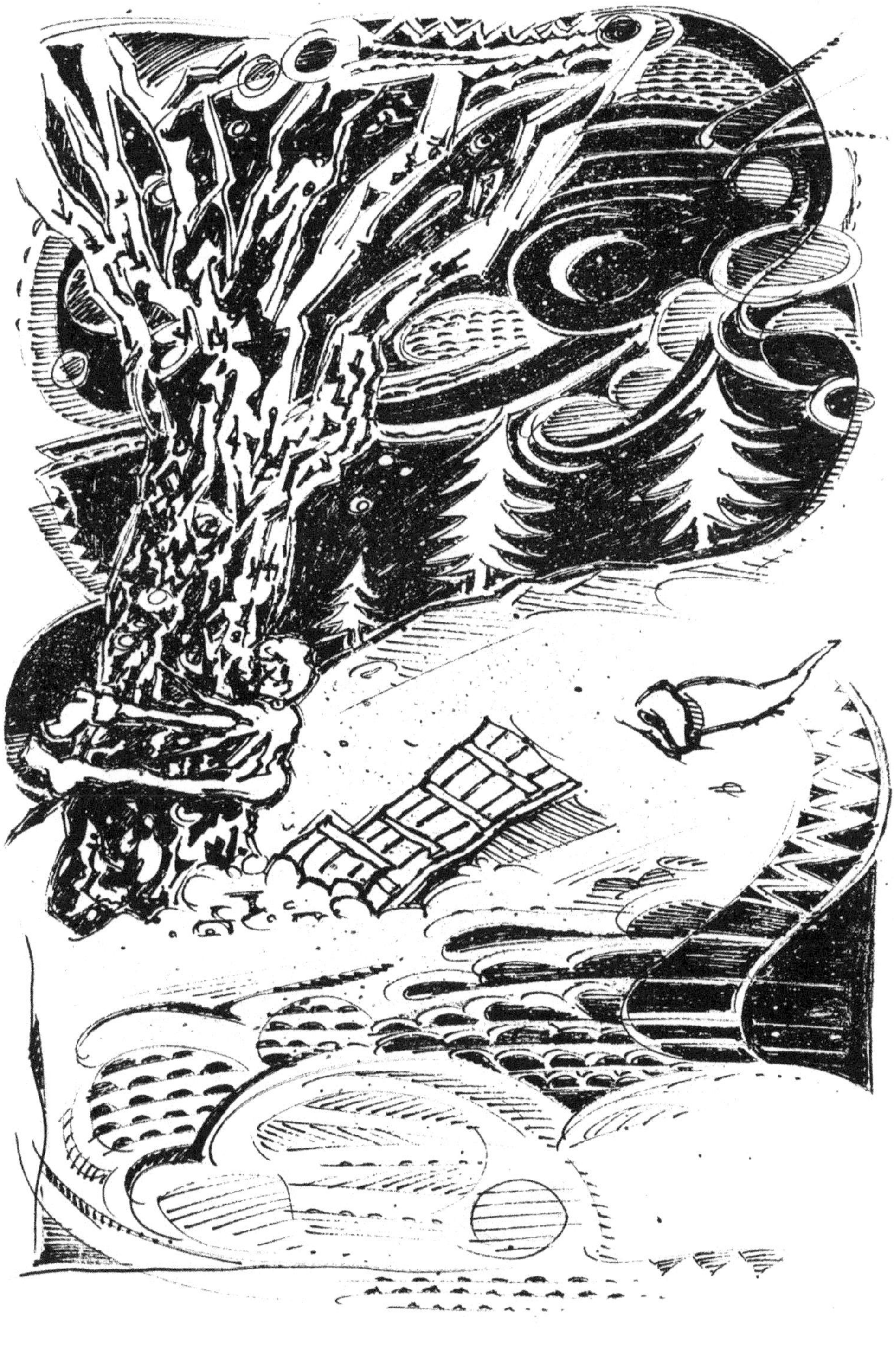

10. CRUSHED BY A CHRISTMAS TREE (THE CAT DID IT)

Of all the predators in the animal world, the cutest is the cat. The best thing about them is this: they don't even need to be malicious to aid you in your goal of reducing the elf population.

Just load O Tannenbaum with an especially twinkly set of lights and leave the base screws nice and loose. Tell your friendly elf spy that the cat may be up to mischief. He will stake out the scene waiting for acts of naughtiness to report back to the North Pole, and this will be his undoing.

It's only a matter of time before your feline friend will attack the lights and bring the whole tree down. Without the slightest hint of ill-will, your kitten's playful ways will lead to one less elf this holiday season.

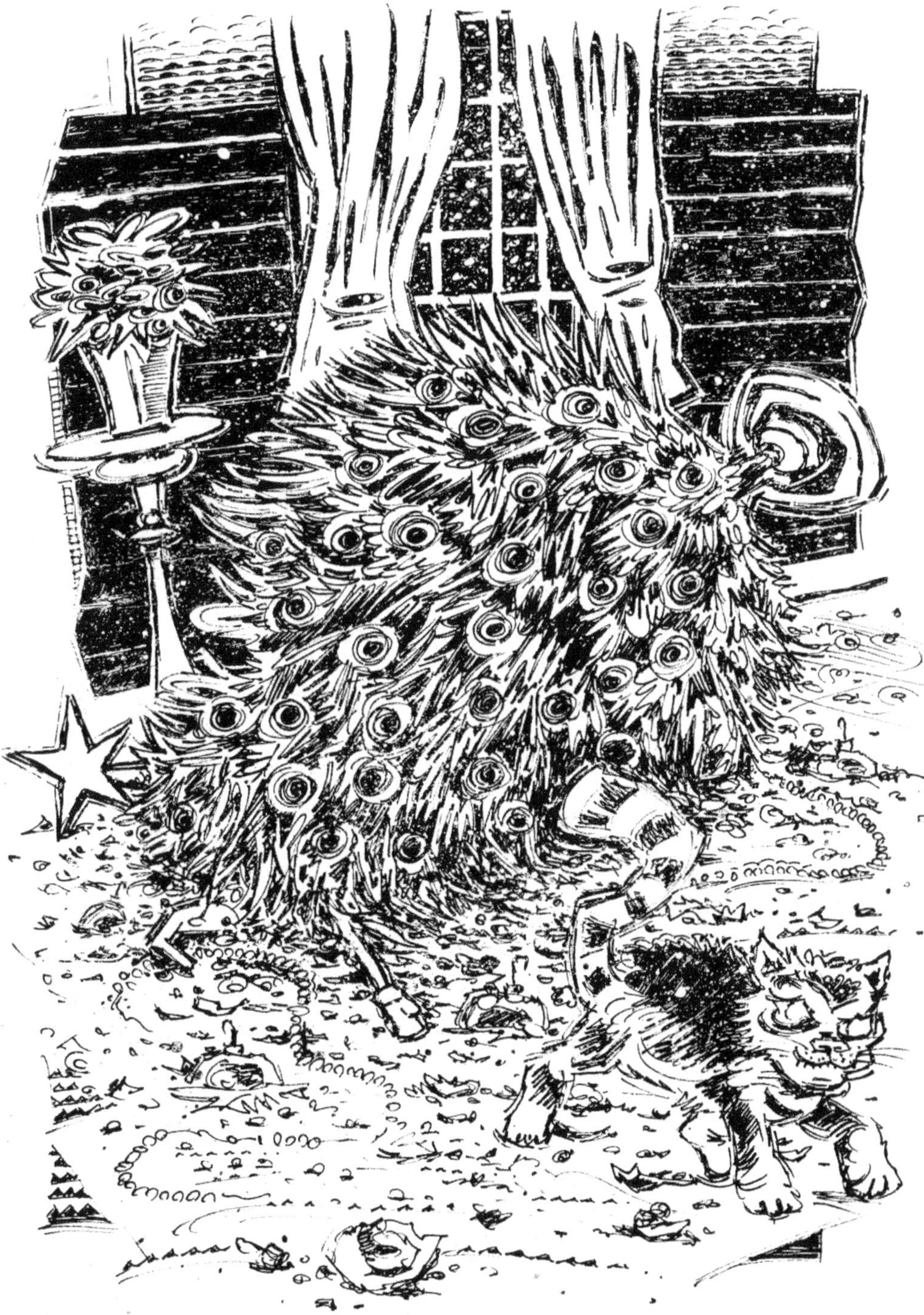

11. KNIT HIM INTO AN UGLY SWEATER

Somewhere along the line, ugly sweaters became a holiday thing. What had been once been kitsch crossed the line into hipster irony. And at that moment, it immediately became marketable: hideous needlepoint-style renditions of snowmen, vile color combinations, extreme tackiness. white turtlenecks popping over crew-necks.

Should you find yourself invited to a party this holiday season and in need of an ugly sweater, here is a piece of advice: Take a regular sweater and weave in an elf. He is, of course, unlikely to survive the process, but he will definitely win accolades at your next Ugly Sweater Party's Ugly Sweater Contest.

Why?

Because there is no uglier sweater possible than one with a real (formerly-) live elf in it.

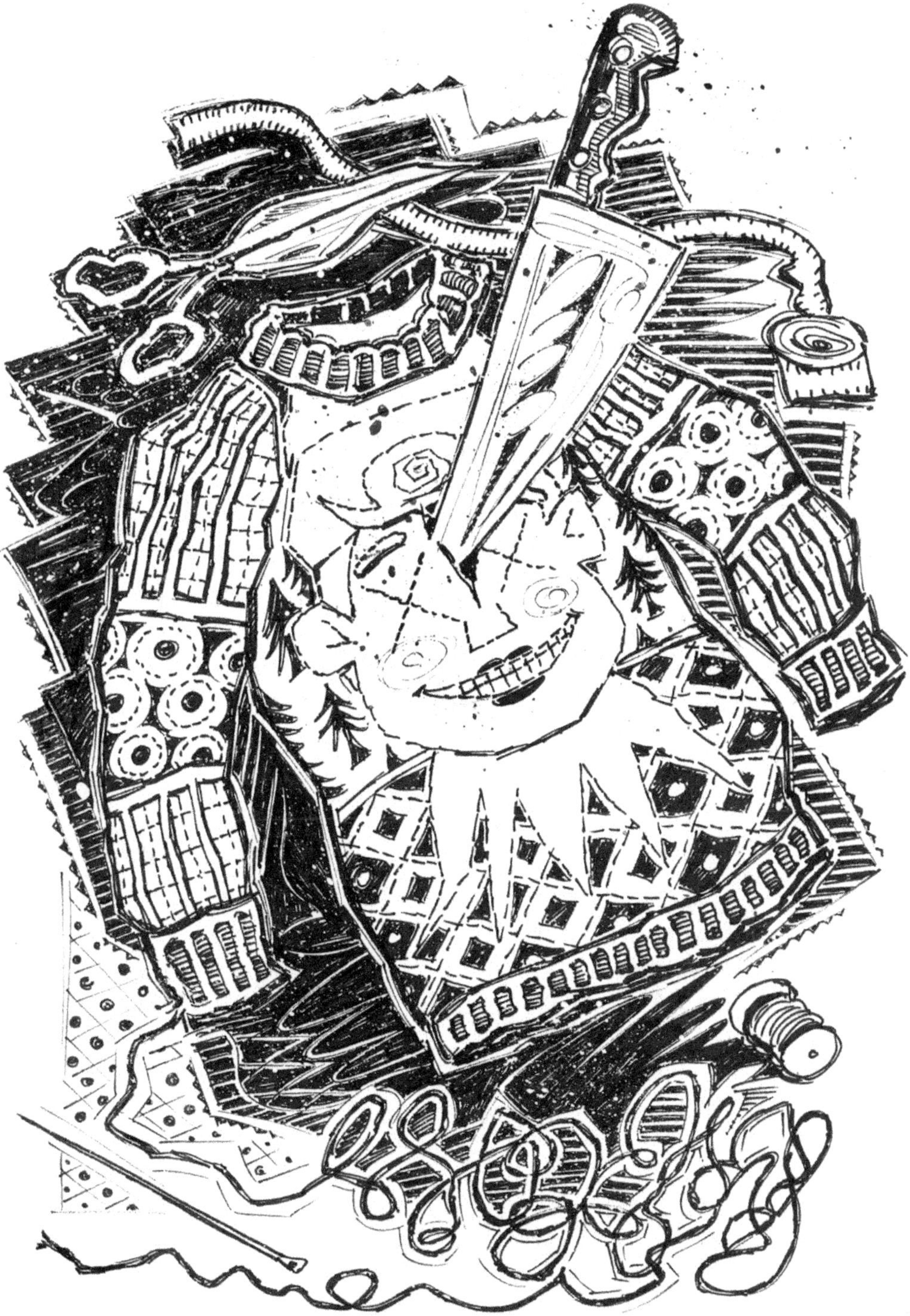

12. WRAPPED AS A GIFT...TO THE GRIM REAPER!

The elf, as a species, is as soft-hearted as it is stupid.

Explain to an elf that the Grim Reaper never gets presents for Christmas, that his job makes him the odd-man out at holiday parties, and you will immediately stimulate the elf's sympathy. Casually mention that all the Grim Reaper really wants for Christmas is an elf - with that the preparation is complete. After the hour or so it takes an elf to put things together, he will volunteer to be wrapped up in an airproof cellophane sheet and delivered at once.

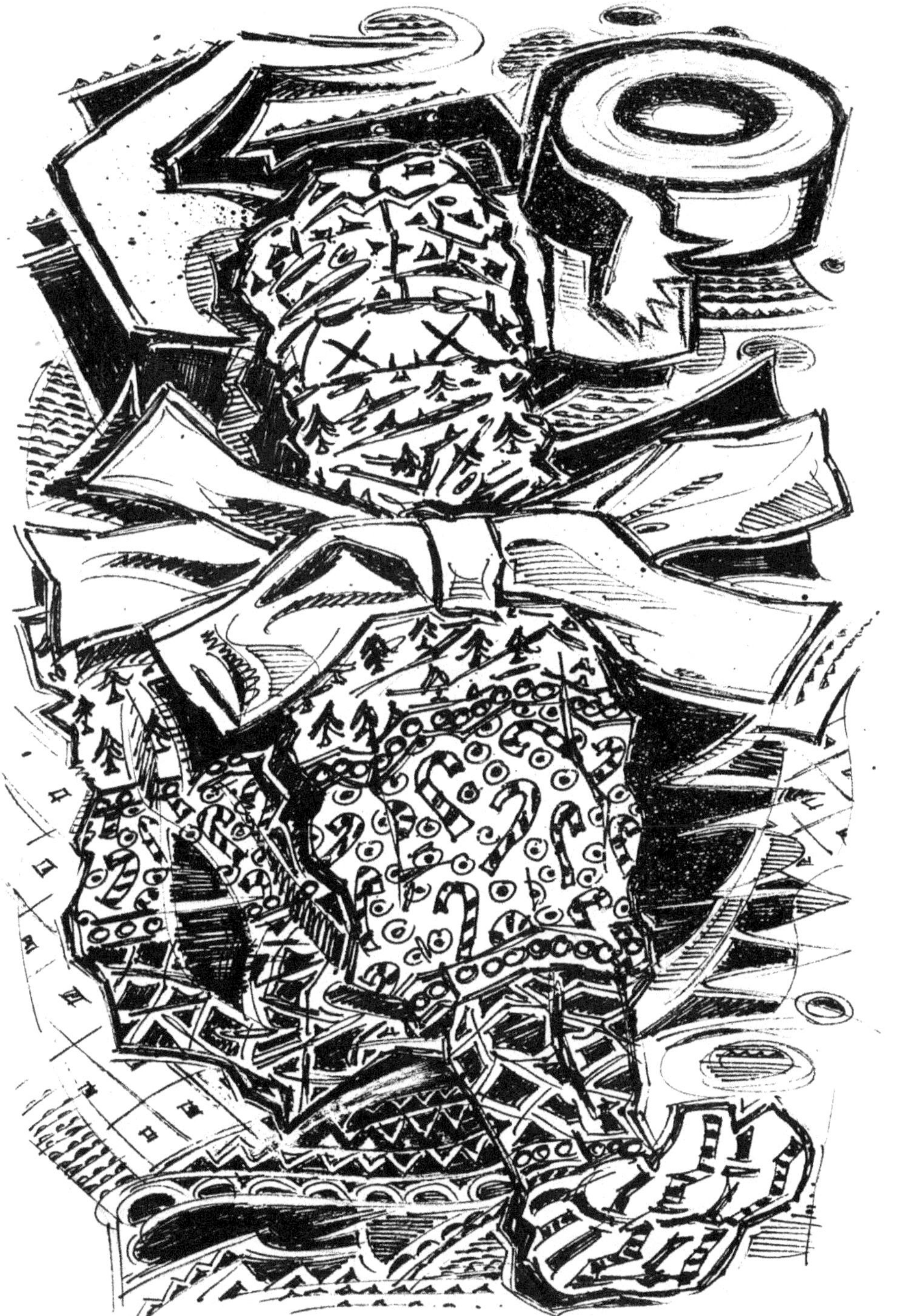

13. FED TO GREMLINS AFTER MIDNIGHT

The 1984 movie Gremlins provides an ideal solution to a growing elf population: A growing population of gremlins. Go to a mysterious backstreet Chinese store and ask for a mogwai. You will receive the following warning:

There are some rules that you've got to follow. First of all, keep him out of the light, he hates bright light, especially sunlight, it'll kill him. Second, don't give him any water, not even to drink. But the most important rule, the rule you can never forget, no matter how much he cries, no matter how much he begs, never feed him after midnight.

...and then you can buy your gremlin. Take it home and put it in a soundproof room in your house. At the stroke of midnight, give your elf a glass of water and plate of cookies and say "Be a dear, take these into the soundproof room."

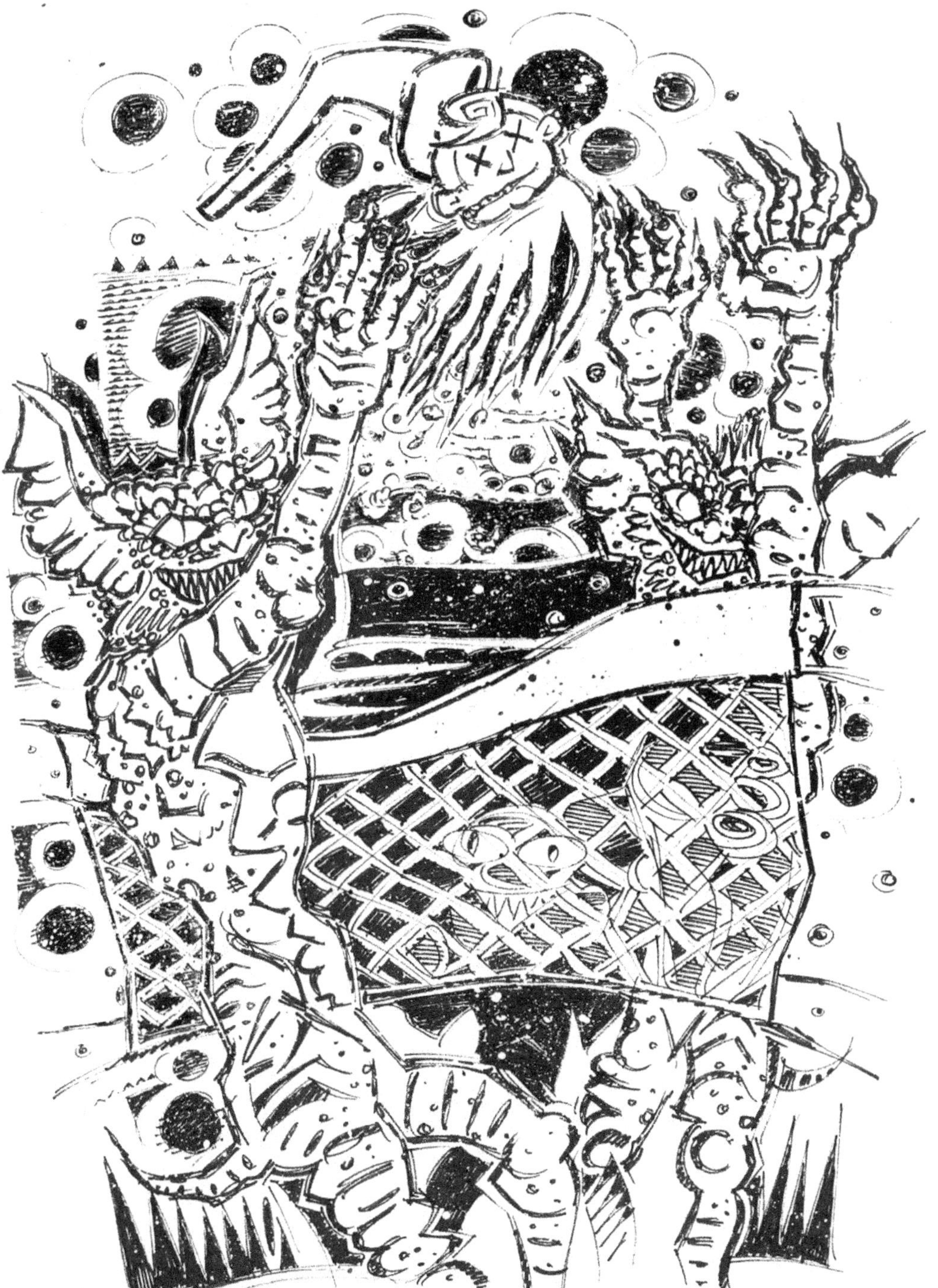

14. LISTEN TO CAROLS ON AN ORGAN PIPE CACTUS

Many of the most beloved songs of Christmas are played on the church organ. This fact can help you to ensnare an unwary elf! They are notoriously gullible creatures, so it should be easy to convince him that an Arizona-based plant called the organ pipe cactus is actually an organ pipe. Here's how.

1. Take your elf on a winter getaway to the beautiful Organ Pipe Cactus National Monument in Ajo, Arizona.
2. Point out one of the beautiful plants that give this National Park its name.
3. Explain that the cactus got its name because if you listen very closely, each plant is gently playing the refrain from Silent Night.
4. Rely on the natural Velcro action of the cactus to ensnare your elf.

If this fails, or your elf is not a fan of religious music, explain that this cactus has a delicious fruit that makes a delightful alternative to cranberry sauce, or a pleasant beverage. All he has to do is climb up and pick the fruit.

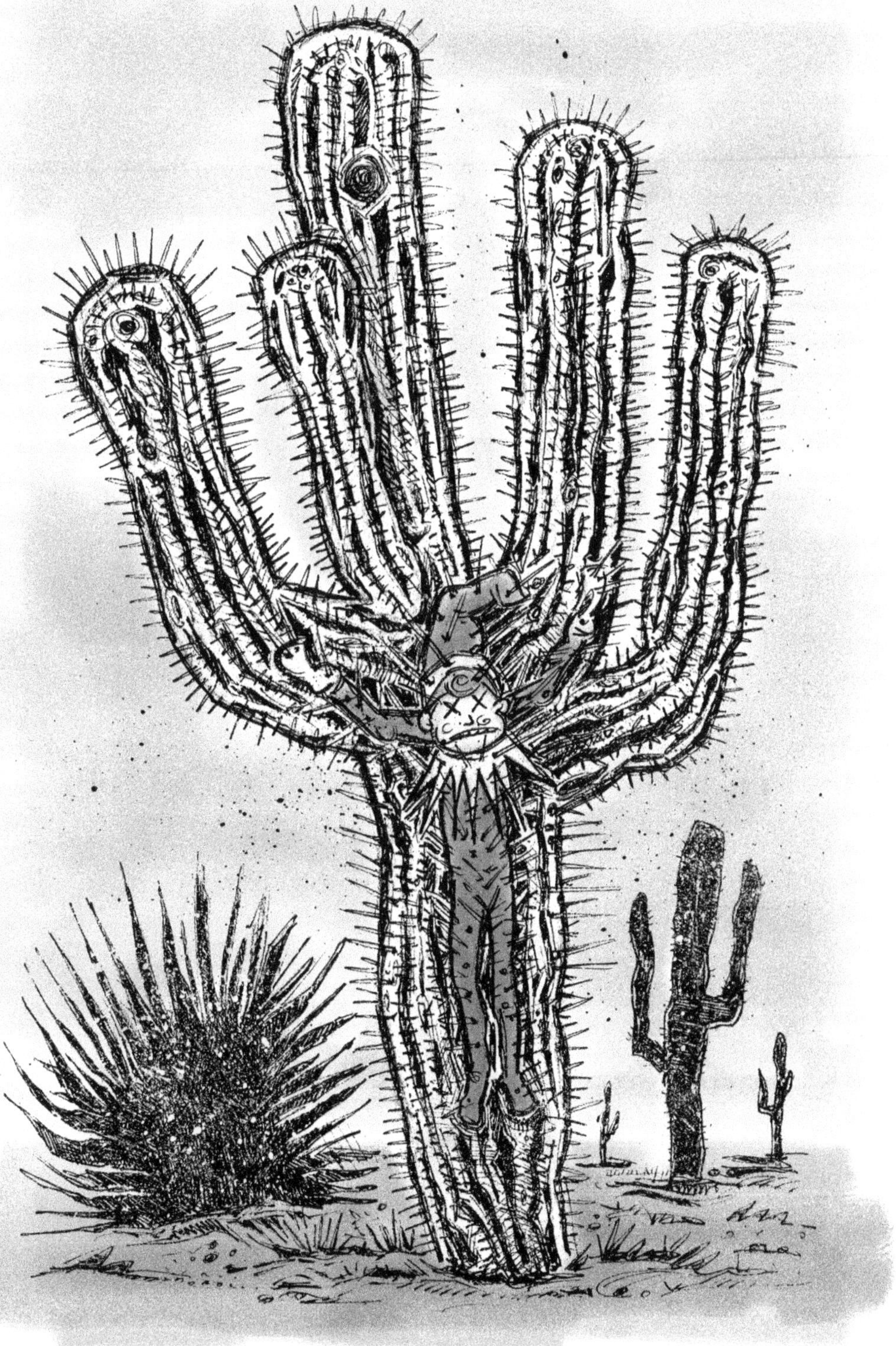

15. ONE WORD: TURDUCKELF

Ingredients:

10 to 12-pound turkey, deboned.

5 to 6-pound duck, completely deboned.

3 to 4-pound chicken, completely deboned (optional).

Your momma's stuffing.

One regular elf.

Make your stuffing according to your momma's secret recipe. Divide it into three parts and put it to one side. Preheat the oven to 300 F.

Spread bread stuffing evenly into turkey cavity. Insert duck. Spread stuffing on top of open duck cavity. Insert chicken.

Ask elf to crawl in and fill the chicken cavity with stuffing. Once the elf is fully inside, skewer the back of the chicken closed. Bring up the sides of the duck to cover the chicken and skewer the duck closed, then skewer the turkey closed.

Wait until all thrashing inside the turduckelf has ended. Remove all skewers except the last one holding the turkey together and place the turduckelf in a heavy roaster. Roast 3 to 4 hours, until meat thermometer inserted in the very center of the chicken or elf stuffing reaches 165 F. Let the turduckelf cool for 30 minutes, then carve and serve.

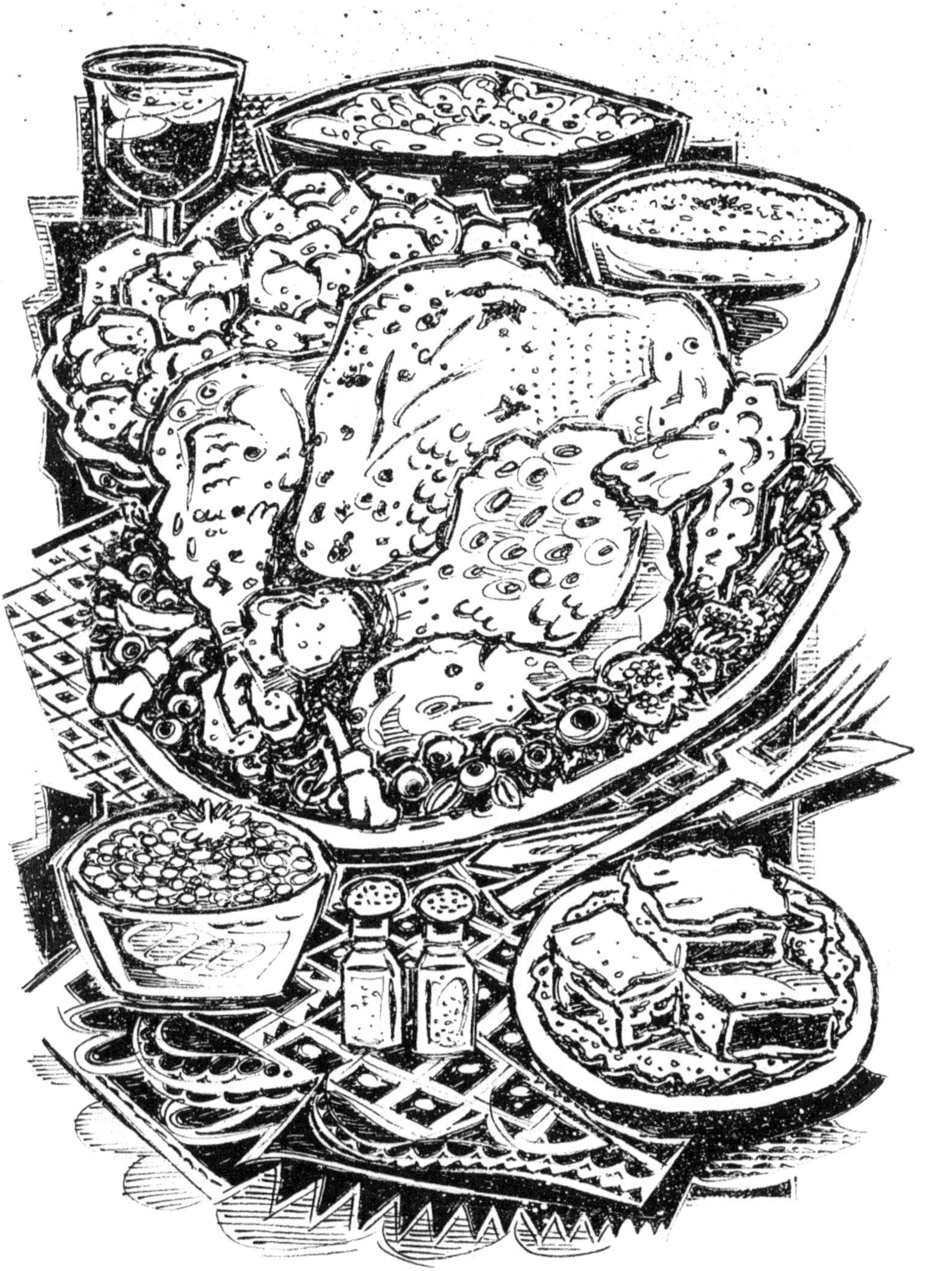

16. HUNG BY THE CHIMNEY WITH CARE

An elf can be a beautiful accessory to any well-appointed home, if he or she is attached to a suitable decorative mount. Here are some tips for getting the perfect elf head wall mounting:

1. Call around your local sporting retailers, hunting clubs, or Brooklyn's famous Morbid Anatomy Museum for taxidermy recommendations.

2. Check out examples of a taxidermist's work before you make an appointment. Can you imagine this person's work on your wall? If not, move on to another taxidermist. People have different tastes in home decor!

3. Once you have found a taxidermist you like, provide your elf's measurements, and ask to see a catalog of suitable mounts.

4. To avoid disappointment, ask to have a written estimate of costs—before you sign a contract!

5. When your mounted elf head arrives, be sure to use a picture hook rated to handle the weight of the mount.

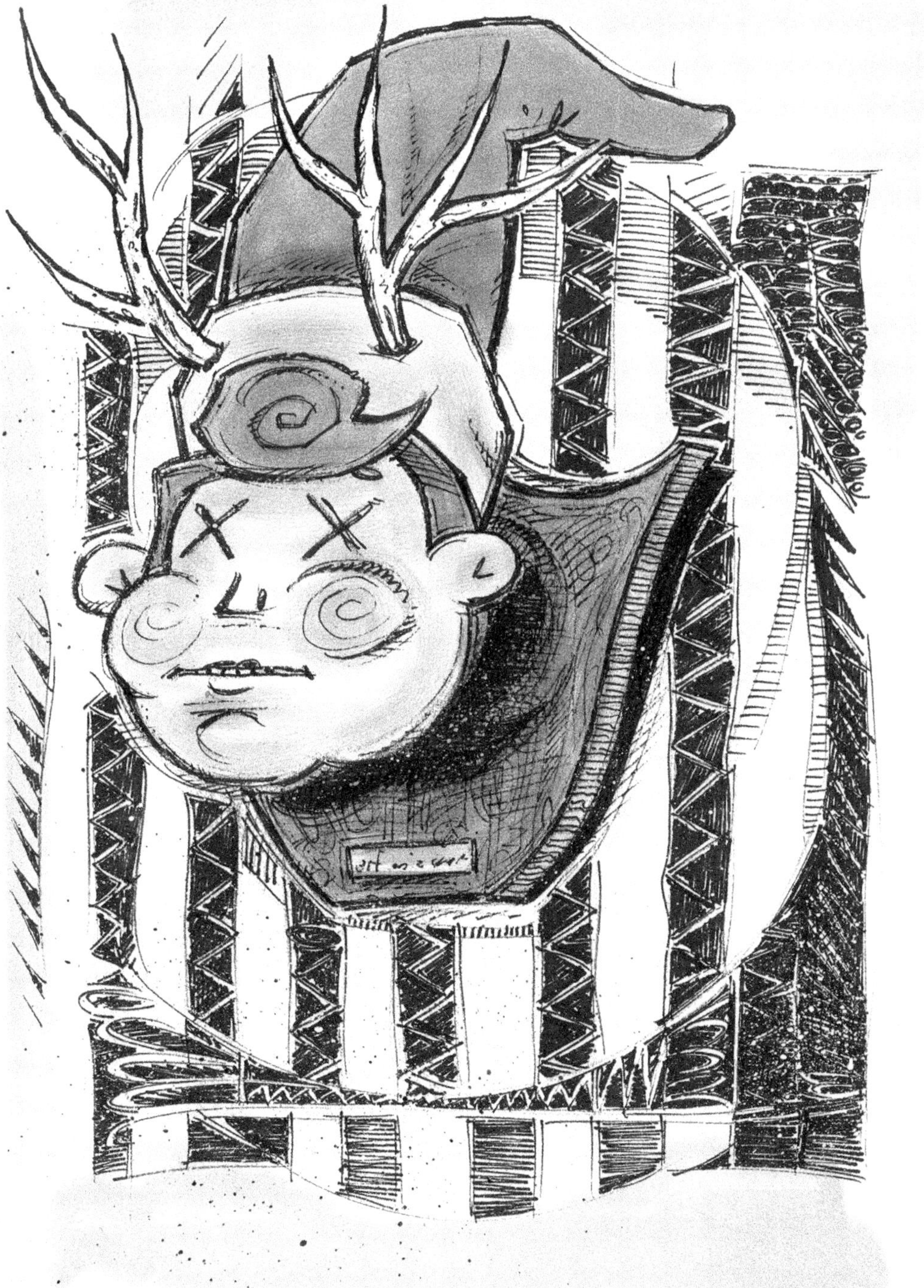

17. MIX A DIRTY ELF MARTINI

Ingredients

1 elf

6 fl. oz. vodka

1 dash dry vermouth

1 fluid ounce brine from olive jar

1 - 4 stuffed green olives

Instructions

1. Place elf in ice bucket with olive in his mouth.
2. In a mixing glass, combine vodka, dry vermouth, brine and remainder of olives.
3. Pour ice into mixing glass.
4. When elf stops twitching, lay him in chilled cocktail glass.
5. To enjoy martini straight, strain into the chilled cocktail glass.
6. To enjoy burying your elf under ice, pour on-the-rocks mixture into chilled cocktail glass.

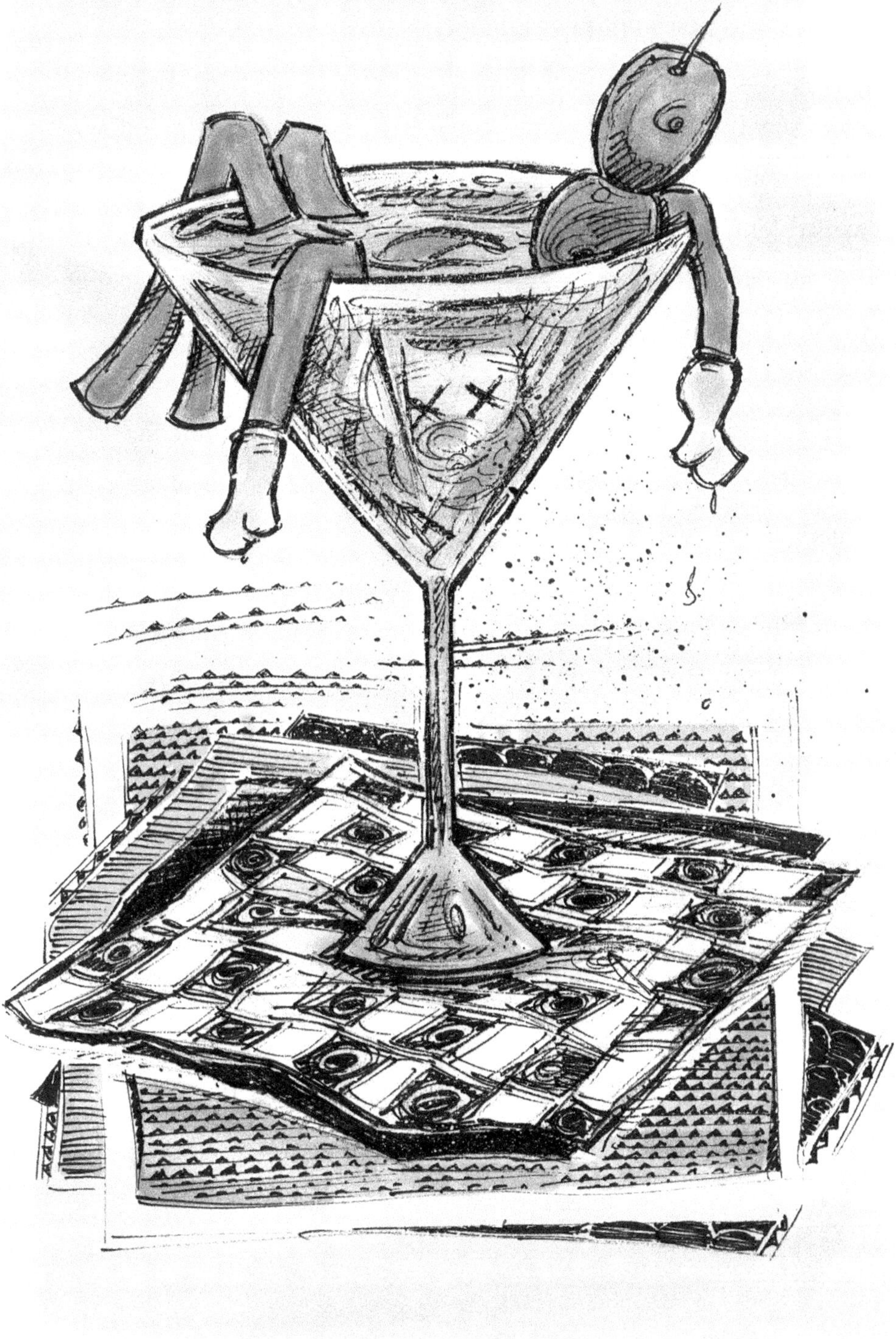

18. DECKED IN THE HALLS

Not every fight is an act of barbarism, say those people who follow the centuries-old traditional of "pugilism." A fan of fisticuffs named John Sholto Douglas published a set of rules for fighting fair, way back in 1867. He even added a little gentlemanly gravitas to the sport by using his royal title the Marquess of Queensbury.

So if you want to avoid accusations of cruelty while pummeling your elf, obey these elf-centric examples of the Marquess of Queensbury's rules:

- If your elfin opponent falls, he must get up unassisted within 10 seconds. You must return to his corner. When the fallen elf is on his legs, the round is to be resumed and continued until the three minutes have expired. If the elf fails to come to the scratch in the 10 seconds allowed, it shall be in the power of the referee to give his award in favour of the non-elf.
- An elf hanging on the ropes in a helpless state, with his toes off the ground, shall be considered down.
- No other elf, reindeer, or Santa's helper to be allowed in the ring during the rounds.
- An elf on one knee is considered down.

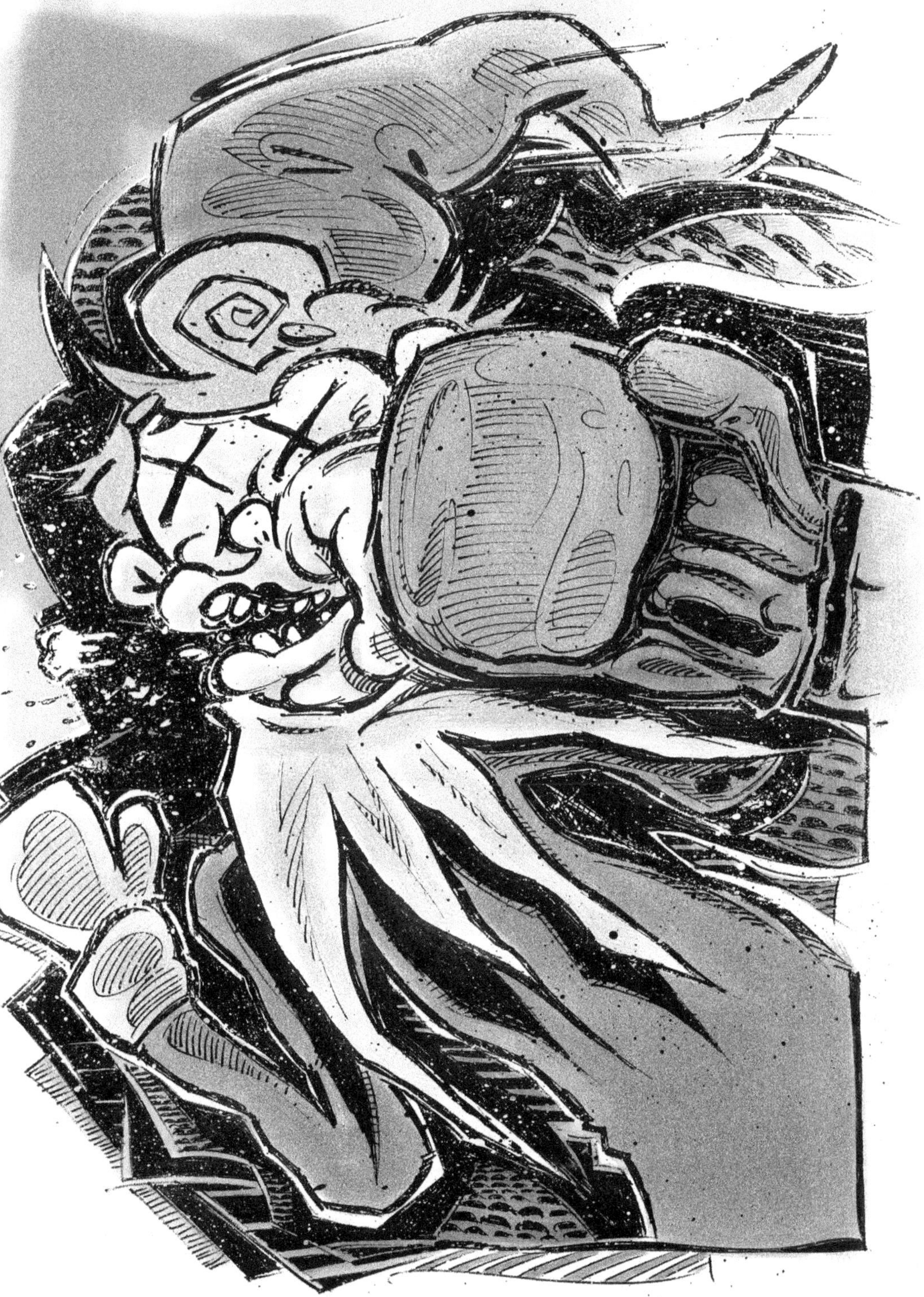

19. CRUSHED BY AN ACME® BRAND ANVIL

While much has been said about the limited value of ACME® Brand equipment for dispatching cartoon birds[1], it can be a formidable weapon against the domestic elf.

The prevailing wisdom on the efficacy of ACME® Brand Anvils boils down to this: They tend to fail in cartoons featuring Wile E. Coyote because most people are rooting for the Road Runner to win.

This can hardly be the case with elves: Nobody wants an elf to survive. So ignore any unfavorable reviews: ACME® Brand Anvils are highly effective against elves because of the laws of cartoon justice: The will of the people always prevails.

[1] *Source: The transcript of Wile E. Coyote vs. the Acme Company, The United States District Court, Southwestern District, Tempe, Arizona Case No. B19293, Judge Joan Kujava, Presiding.*

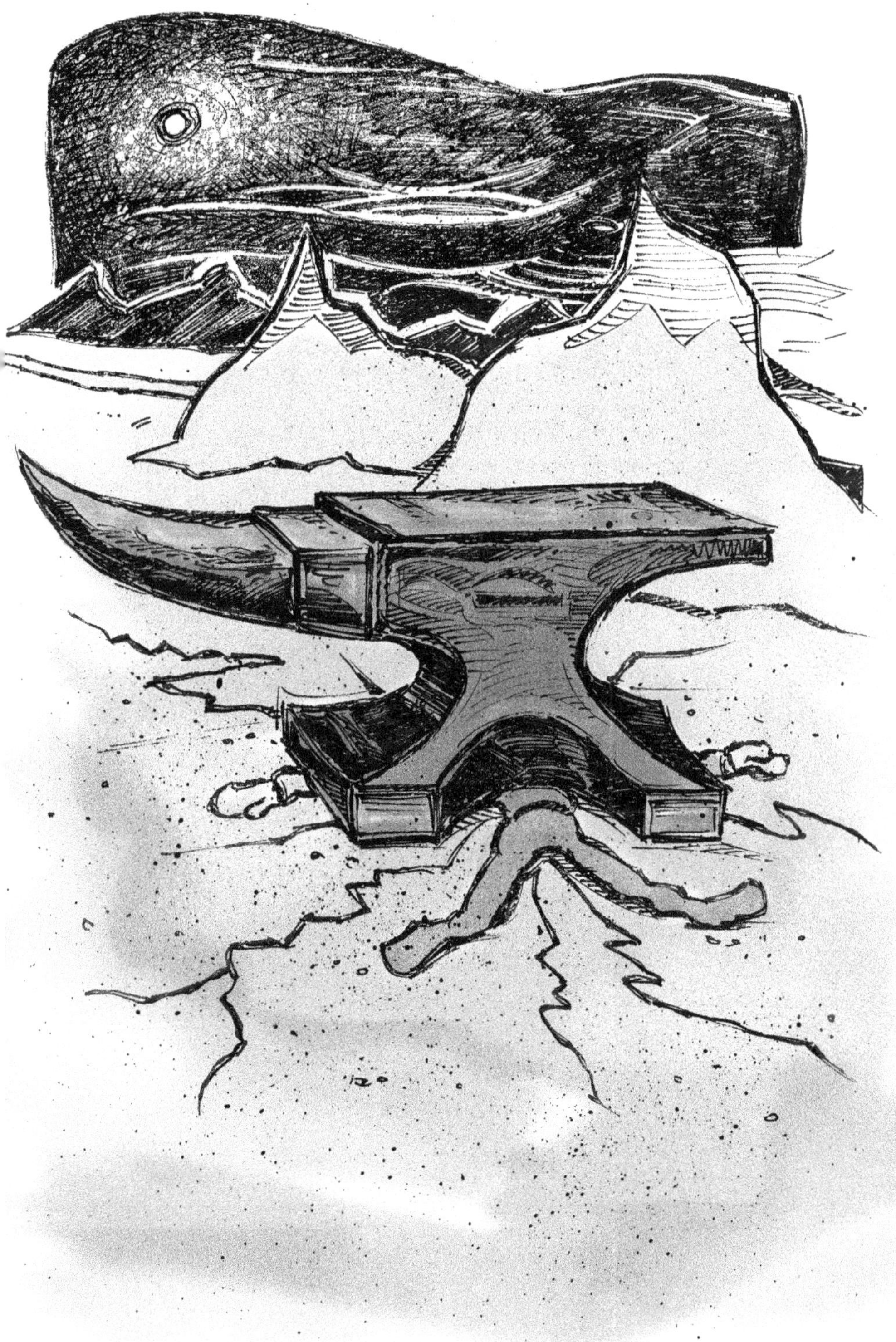

20. ABANDON HIM IN ROSWELL, NEW MEXICO

Elves are intrepid creatures that make the nightly trip back to the North Pole to deliver the results of their daily espionage to Santa. But they are also notoriously bad at finding their way home. Use this fact against them!

1. Reprogram the elfin Global Positioning software to take him to Area 54 in Roswell, NM, instead of to the North Pole
2. Let the aliens take care of the rest.

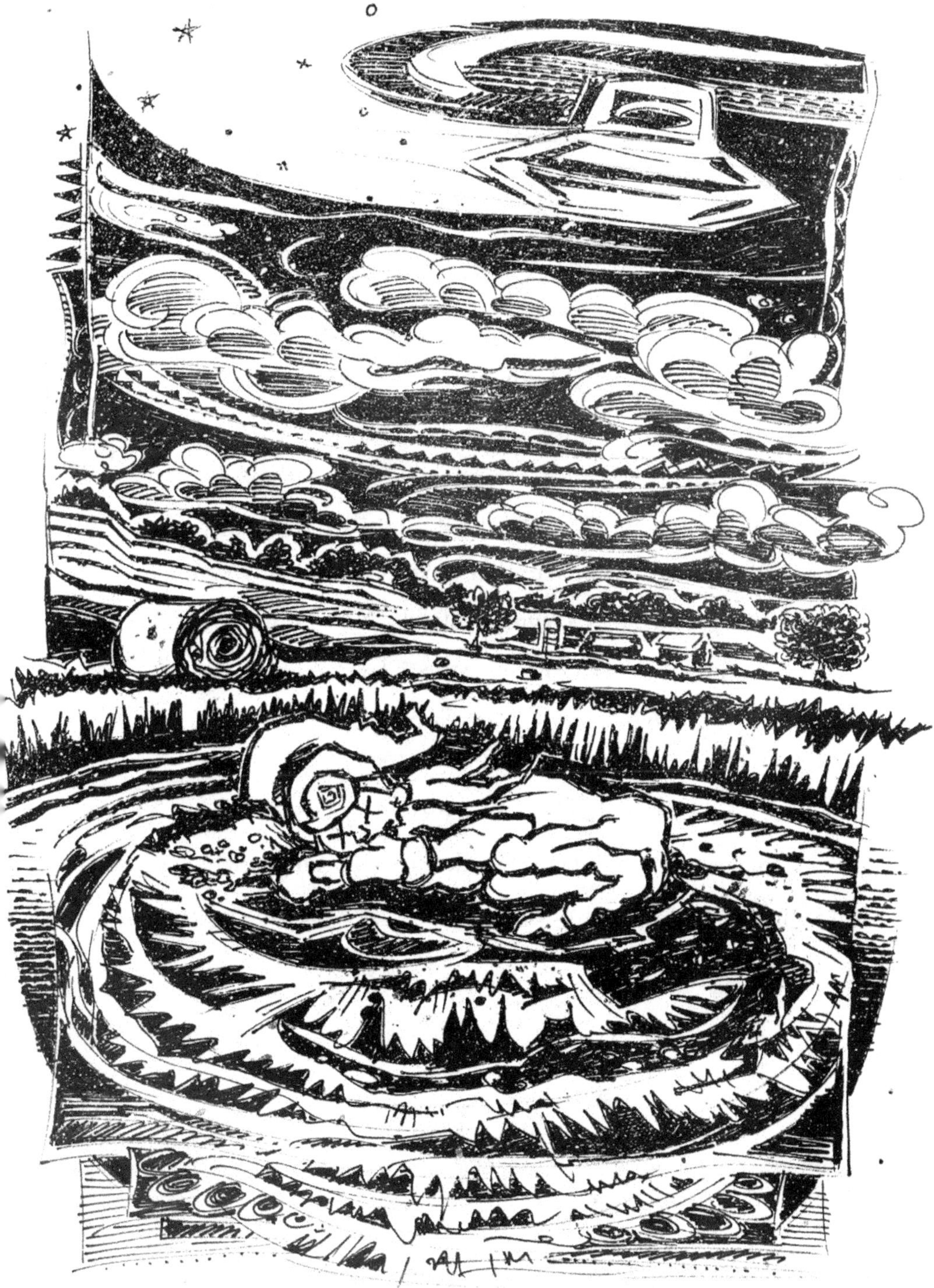

21. ENCOURAGED TO SWIM AT HIS OWN RISK

As we know, the elf travels frequently to report his findings to Santa at the North Pole. Alter his travel plans in this way:

Print out directions to the North Pole from the last-known location of your elf. Make sure that the directions route your elf through the waters of the Cayman Islands, New South Wales, or Amity Island, New York. These locations feature prominently in either Jaws or the Discovery Channel's Shark Week.

Under cover of night the elf may not see the Swim at Your Own Risk signs posted on the beaches nearby. Or perhaps he will, but simply ignore them and continue to follow his directions...

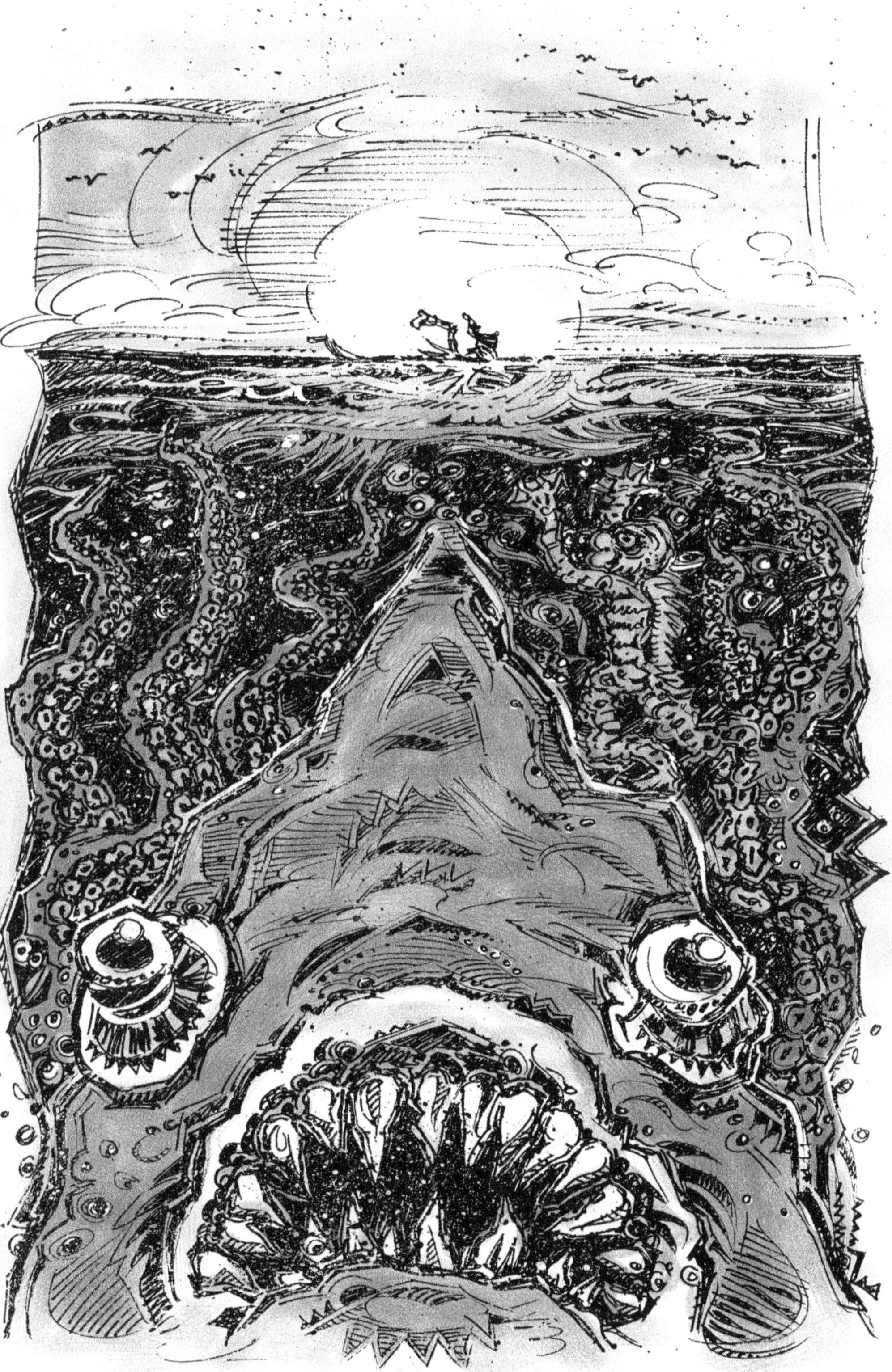

22. USE AS THE GRINCH'S TOOTHBRUSH

All the Whos down in Whoville
Berated the Grinch
Whose teeth were all covered
With plaque by the inch.

"Hey Grinchy!" They cried.
"There is no time to waste!
Crack open this tube
Of the finest toothpaste"

The Grinch grabbed an Elf
And all in a rush
Squirted paste on his face
And proceeded to brush.

He scrubbed and he scrubbed
And his mouth became fresh,
But that wee Elfy beast
Went the way of all flesh.

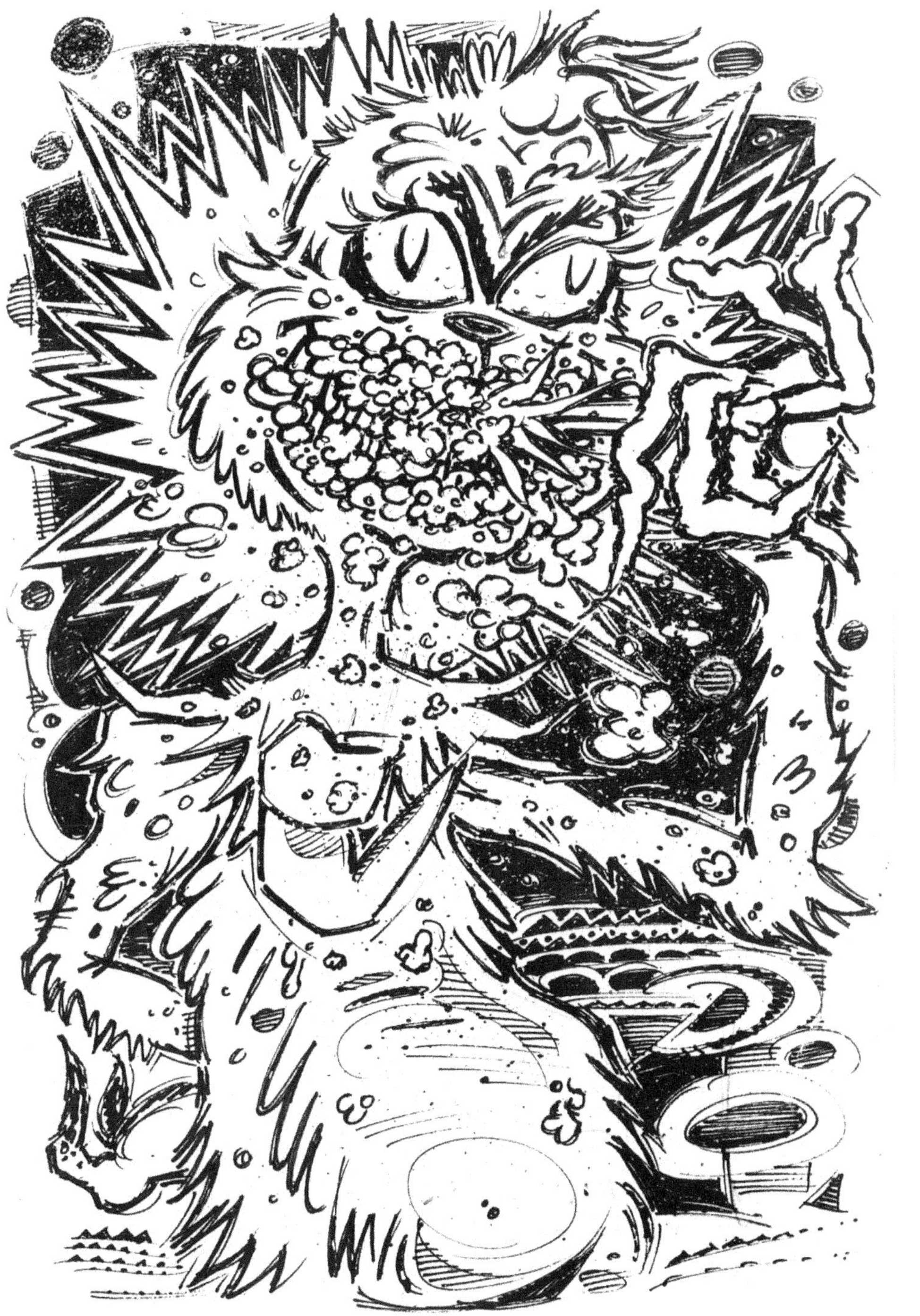

23. MIX HIM UP WITH DOGFOOD

Our best friend and most loyal companion, the dog, can be instrumental in controlling the elf population. Consider these two facts: First, dogs do not have a highly developed sense of taste. Second, dogs are omnivores. Consequently, they will eat almost anything placed before them.

This simple method takes advantage of these canine factoids. Simply bury any spare elves you discover in a heaping bowl of dog food. Then take your dog on a nice long walk to build up a healthy appetite. This should ensure a successful outcome.

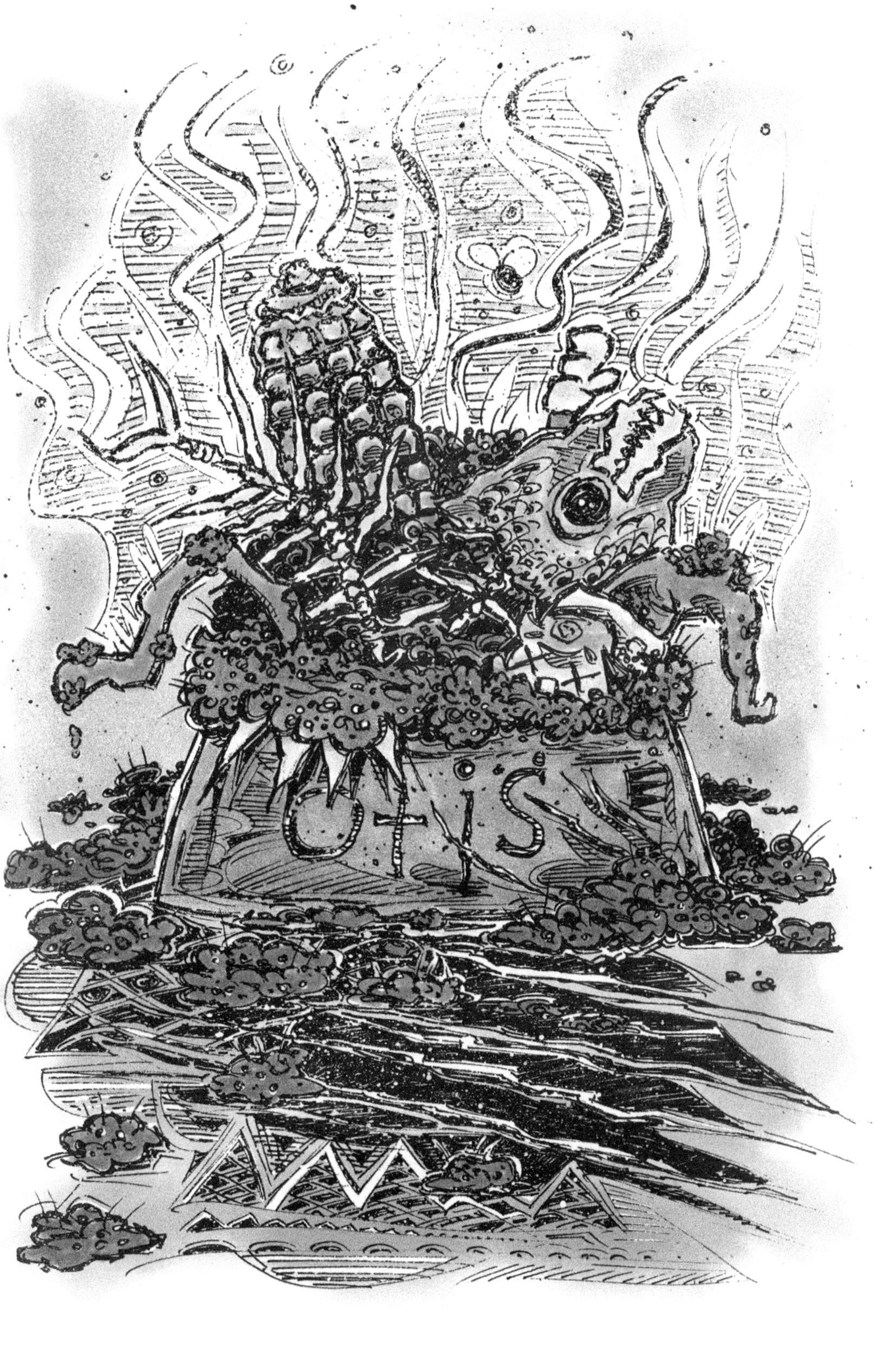

24. TRAMPLED BY THE ABOMINABLE SNOWMAN

The smallest shoe size that would fit an adult Abominable Snowman is a size 20 extra-wide fitting (14 inches long by 6.5 inches wide). That is easily enough to crush an elf, but an Abominable Snowman's 11-foot running stride is enormously wide. Even if manage to get an elf into the path of a sprinting yeti, odds favor the elf not being touched at all.

Therefore, the most surefire technique to ensure a good Snowman trampling fate for your elf is thus: Stake him flat on the ground near a large herd of Abominable Snowmen, sneak around to the other side of the herd, and make a series of loud noises to start a stampede.

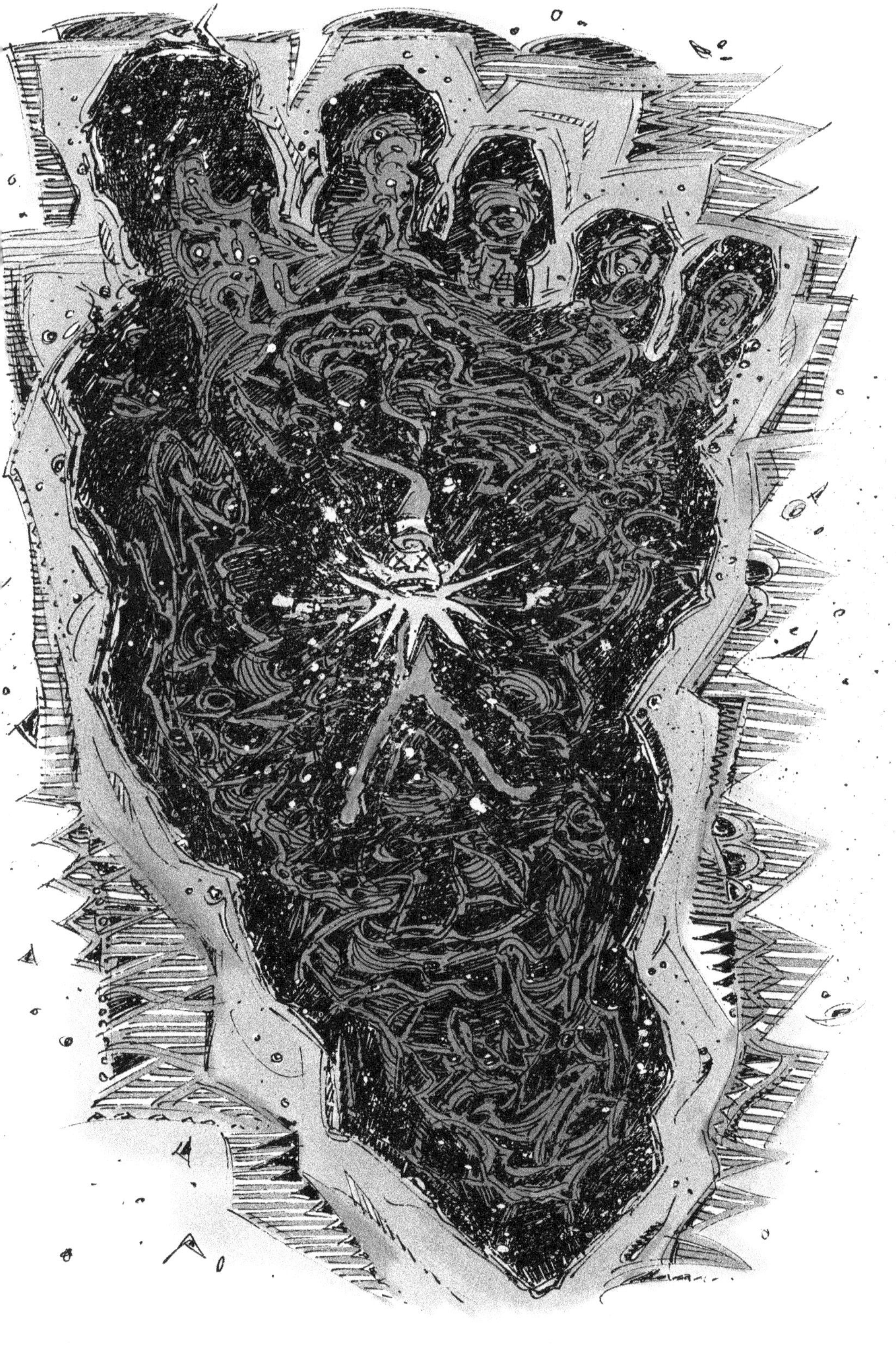

25. TELL AN OWL HE'S A MESSAGE TO HOGWARTS

The owl's reputation for being a wise old bird is completely inaccurate. Owls are remarkably stupid, like most birds, and without three advantages in their favor, they would have died out years ago:

1. They can locate their prey in the dark
2. They can swallow their prey whole, regurgitating any bits they can't digest.
3. They have the exclusive contract to act as mail carriers to schools of witchcraft and wizardry.

In spite of their stupidity, owls are vicious predators and one may count on them to help address the problem of elves. Give an owl an elf, say it is a letter to young wizard. Wave goodbye to the elf as he is carried off, gripped by sharp talons, into the night. If the owl gets him to Hogwarts, he won't get him there alive.

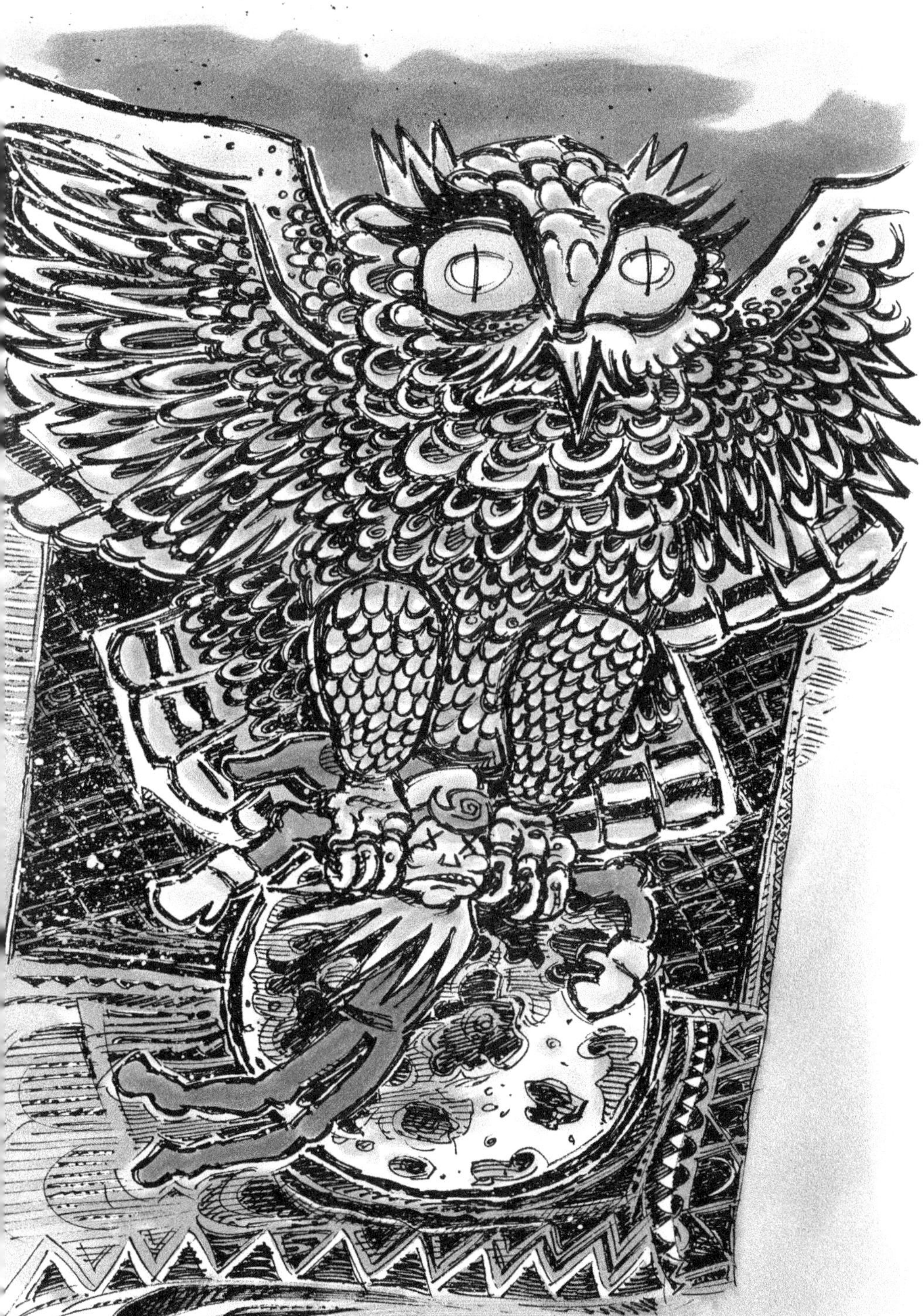

26. MAKE A SEVERED SNOW ANGEL

Making snow angels is fun. Everyone thinks so. So you won't have any trouble persuading your intended elf victim to give it a whirl.

And if he asks why you're carrying a pair of scissors, you can always claim that you're going to wrap presents later.

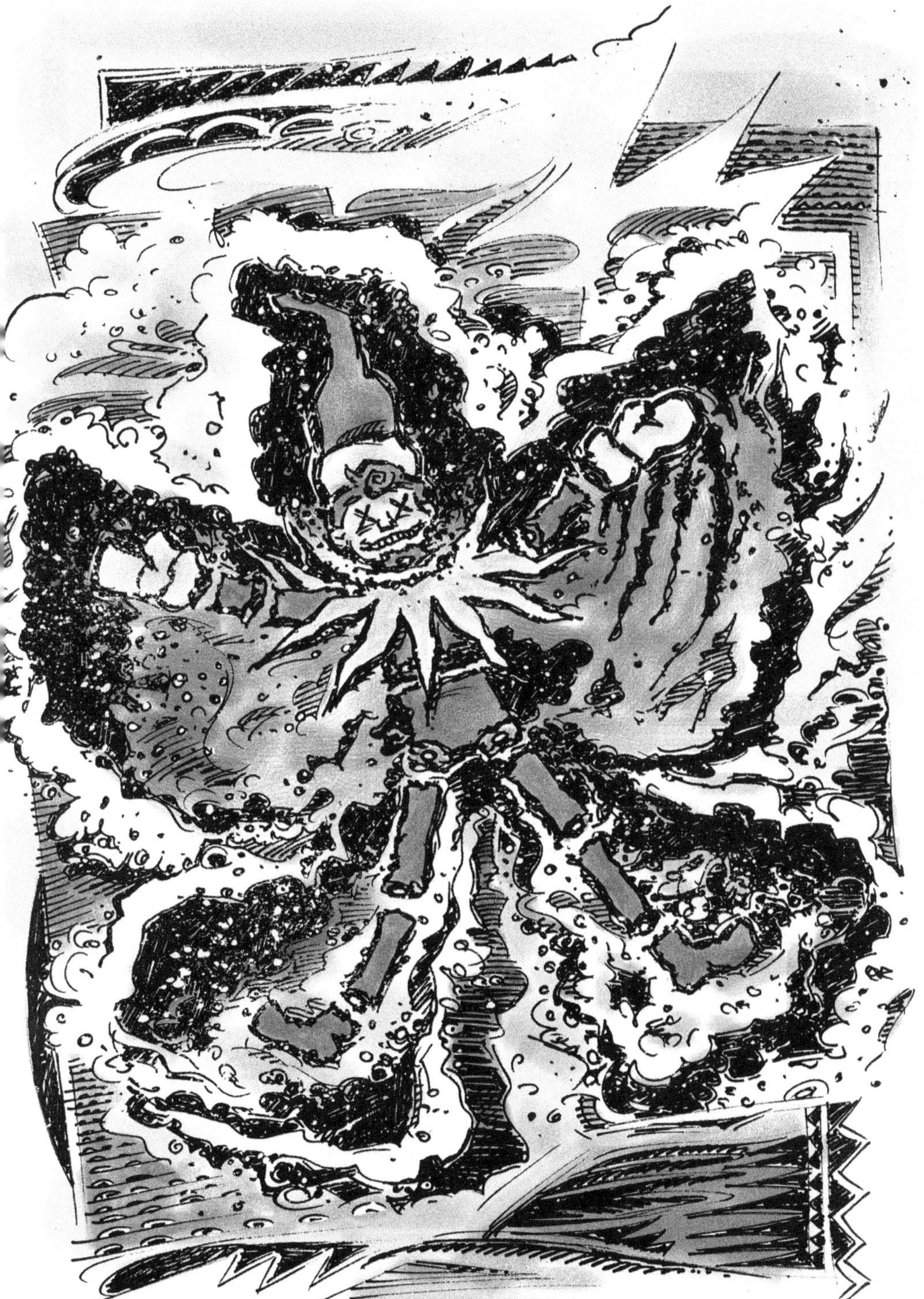

27. TOSS HIM OUT WITH THE FRUITCAKE

The fruitcake is the worst gift ever given at Christmastime: an indigestible invention, trotted out to the dismay of all who witness it; too sweet, too dense, and too widely despised to be enjoyed by festive revelers.

The same criticisms apply to the elf.

Save yourself the anguish and toss them into the dumpster together, tied together with a length of tinsel. Do you need more justification for using this method? This single method rids you of not one but two perennial nuisances!

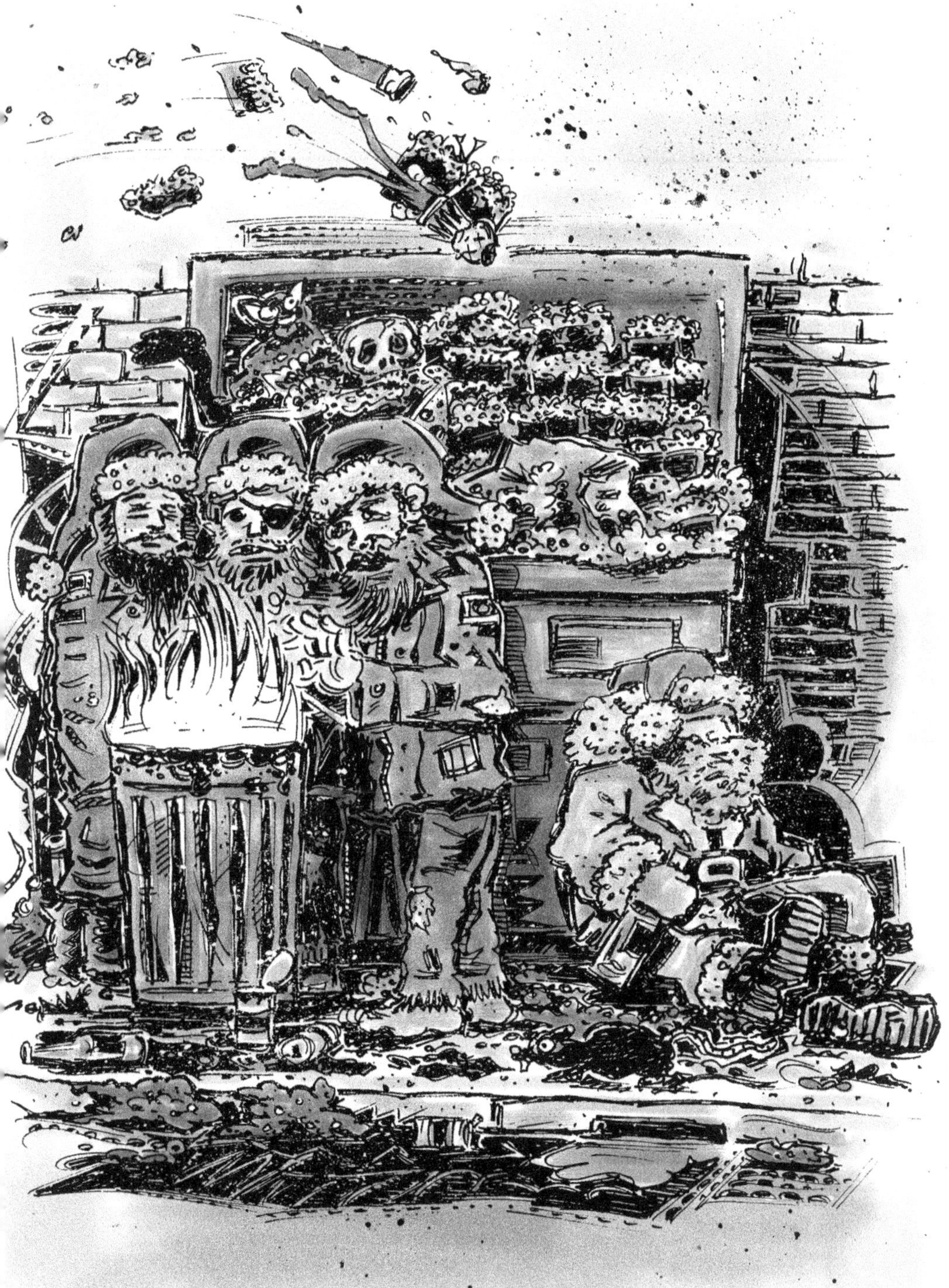

28. BOILED WITH HIS OWN PUDDING

"If I could work my will," said Scrooge indignantly, "Every idiot who goes about with 'Merry Christmas' on his lips, should be boiled with his own pudding…"

Stave I, A Christmas Carol (1843). Charles Dickens.

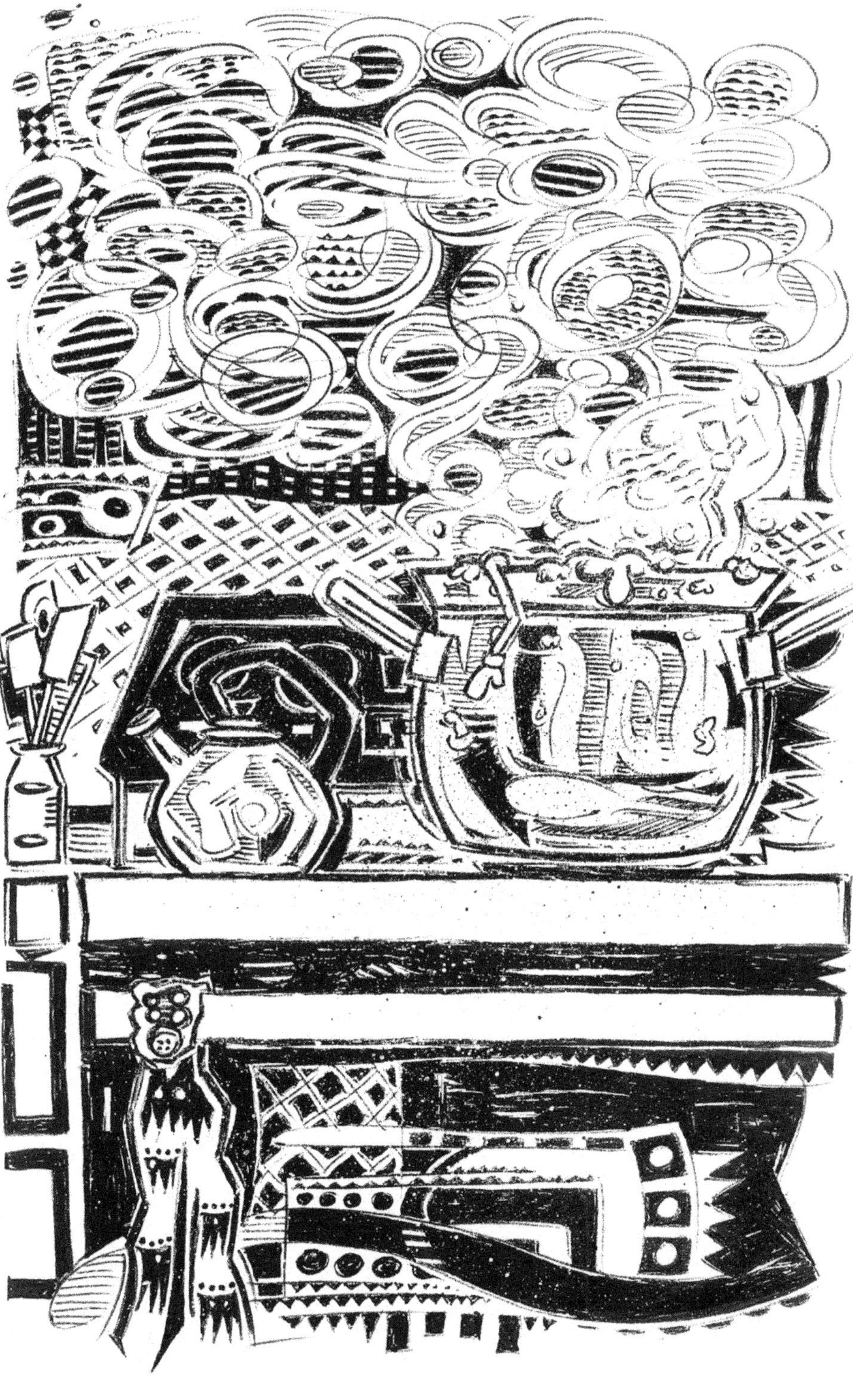

29. BURIED WITH A STAKE OF HOLLY THROUGH HIS HEART

"If I could work my will," said Scrooge indignantly, "Every idiot who goes about with 'Merry Christmas' on his lips, should be boiled with his own pudding, and buried with a stake of holly through his heart. He should!"

Stave I, A Christmas Carol (1843). Charles Dickens.

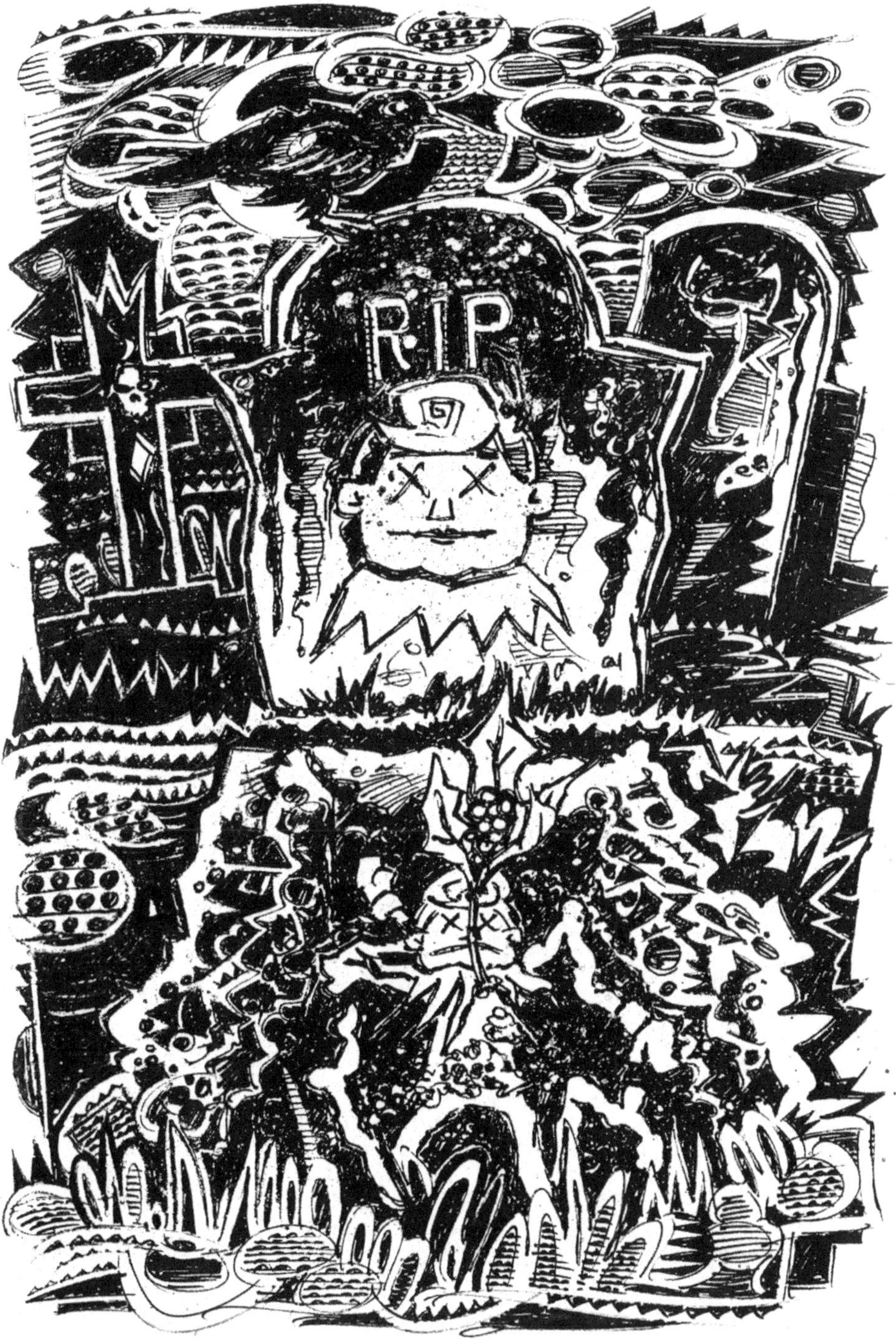
R.I.P

30. MAKE AN ELF O'LANTERN

The common or garden elf is too small and stringy to provide illumination for a whole house, but if tossed into a carved pumpkin, elves can catch fire from the tea light inside and in the right conditions can build up to a good-sized blaze in minutes.

This works especially well if the Elf is dipped into oil or tiki torch fluid beforehand.

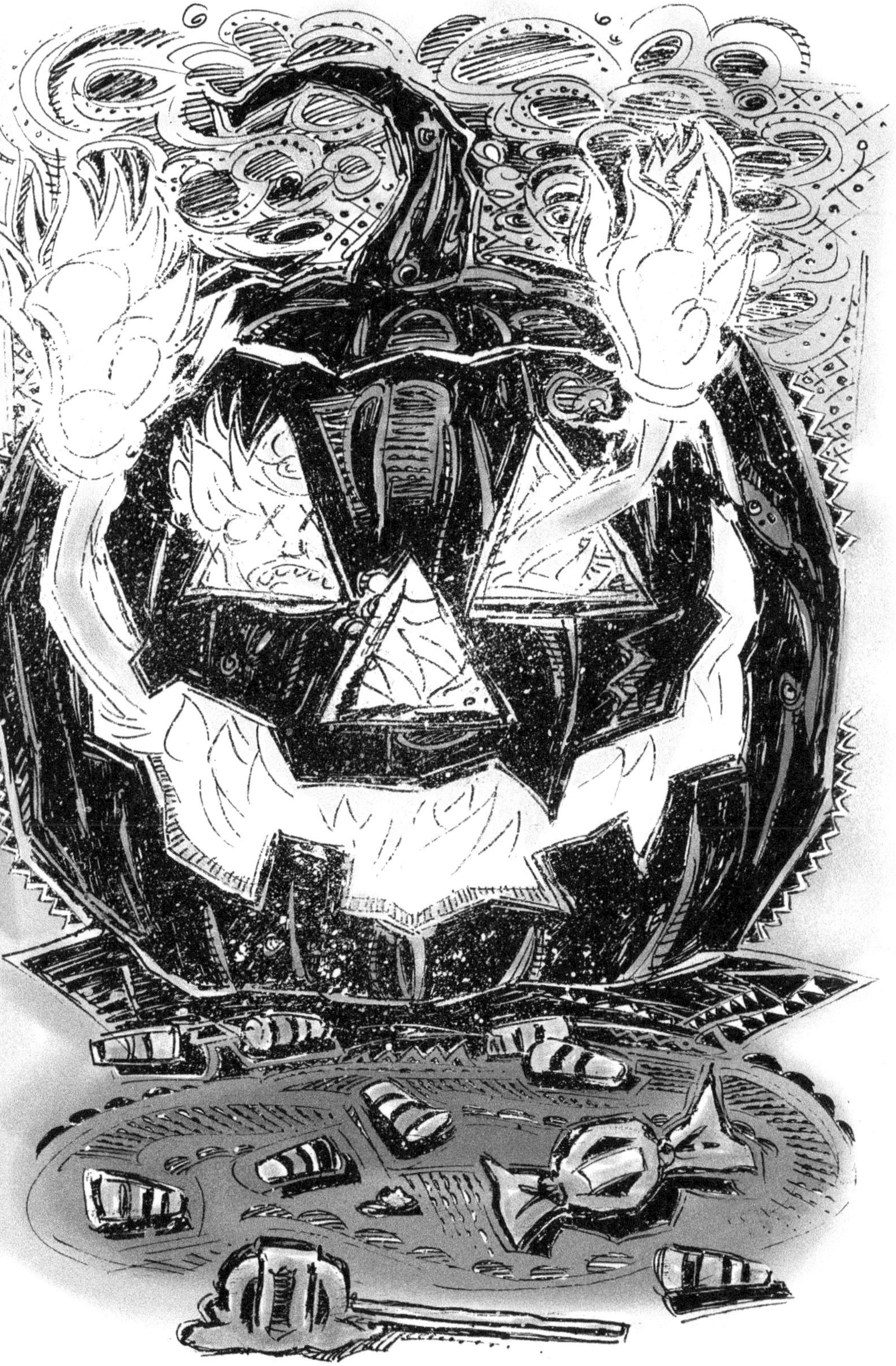

31. PUT HIM IN A SNOWGLOBE

The Viennese company that holds the oldest patent for snowglobes, Wiener Schneekugel, manufactures 350 hand-crafted designs. None of the company's designs includes an elf. But don't let this hold you back. Where human knowledge fails, rely on elfin ingenuity.

Elves are notoriously vain and self-absorbed, as the coy eyes-averted smirk on their little plastic faces will tell. The easiest way to get one into a snowglobe is to persuade him that M. Night Shyamalan is planning a remake of Citizen Kane. The great director wants to feature an elf in the opening scene, where Charles Foster Kane whispers "Rosebud" at a snowglobe and dies. This shot at stardom will get the elf to do all the work.

Merry Christmas

32. USE HIM AS SHOELACES

In many cultures, stockings are not hung by the chimney with care on Christmas Eve. Instead, boots are left by the front door the night before St. Nicholas' Day, December 5th. This festive footwear tradition has the makings of a fiendish elf disposal technique.

In a quest to make sporty footwear into a fashion item in the go-go 1980s, the cobbling industry invented snazzy shoelaces: Neon colors, tiger stripes, zebra stripes, geometric patterns, and emblazoned with cartoon characters.

Convince some of your short-sighted, hard-of-hearing elderly relatives that the long limbs of your elf are the latest style in fashion shoelaces, and ask them to lace them in the boots of their grandchildren. The elfin protests will fall upon literally deaf ears, and the elf population counter will decrease accordingly.

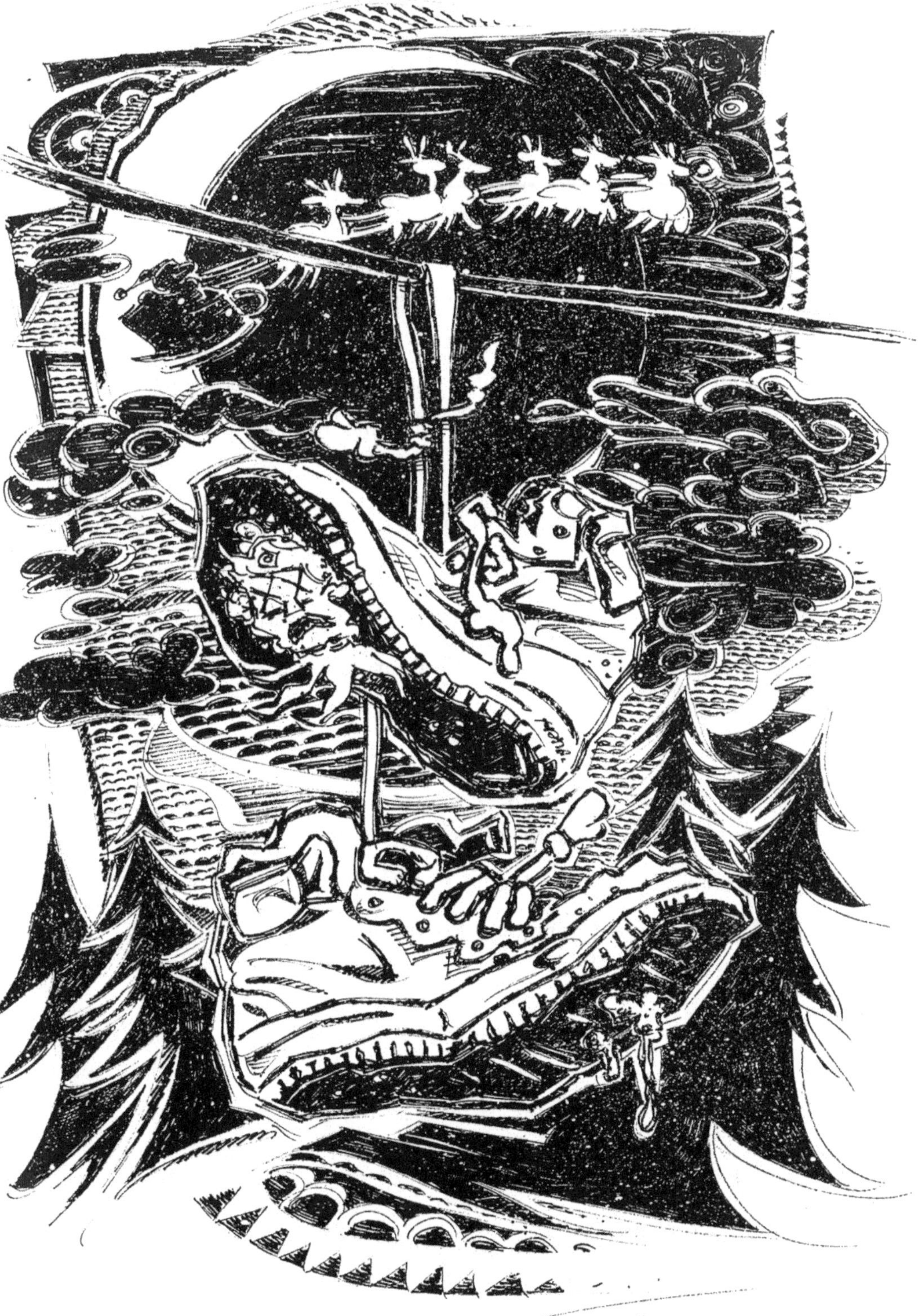

33. KISSED TO DEATH UNDER THE MISTLETOE

In Norse mythology, the god Baldur the Beautiful was granted immunity from anything the gods could imagine as weapons. But the jealous trickster god Loki had a better imagination than most, and made a deadly weapon out of mistletoe. And he persuaded one of his compadres to throw it at Baldur's heart for a joke. Naturally, it killed him. Baldur's mother Frigga wept tears of mistletoe berries, which resurrected the dead Baldur. She was so pleased, she blessed mistletoe and promised that anyone who passed under it would get kissed.

Let's bring back the mistletoe as a deadly weapon this holiday season: Tell all the gods of Asgard to come by and bestow a kiss on your elf. By the time Thor comes by, the smug little critter will be doomed.

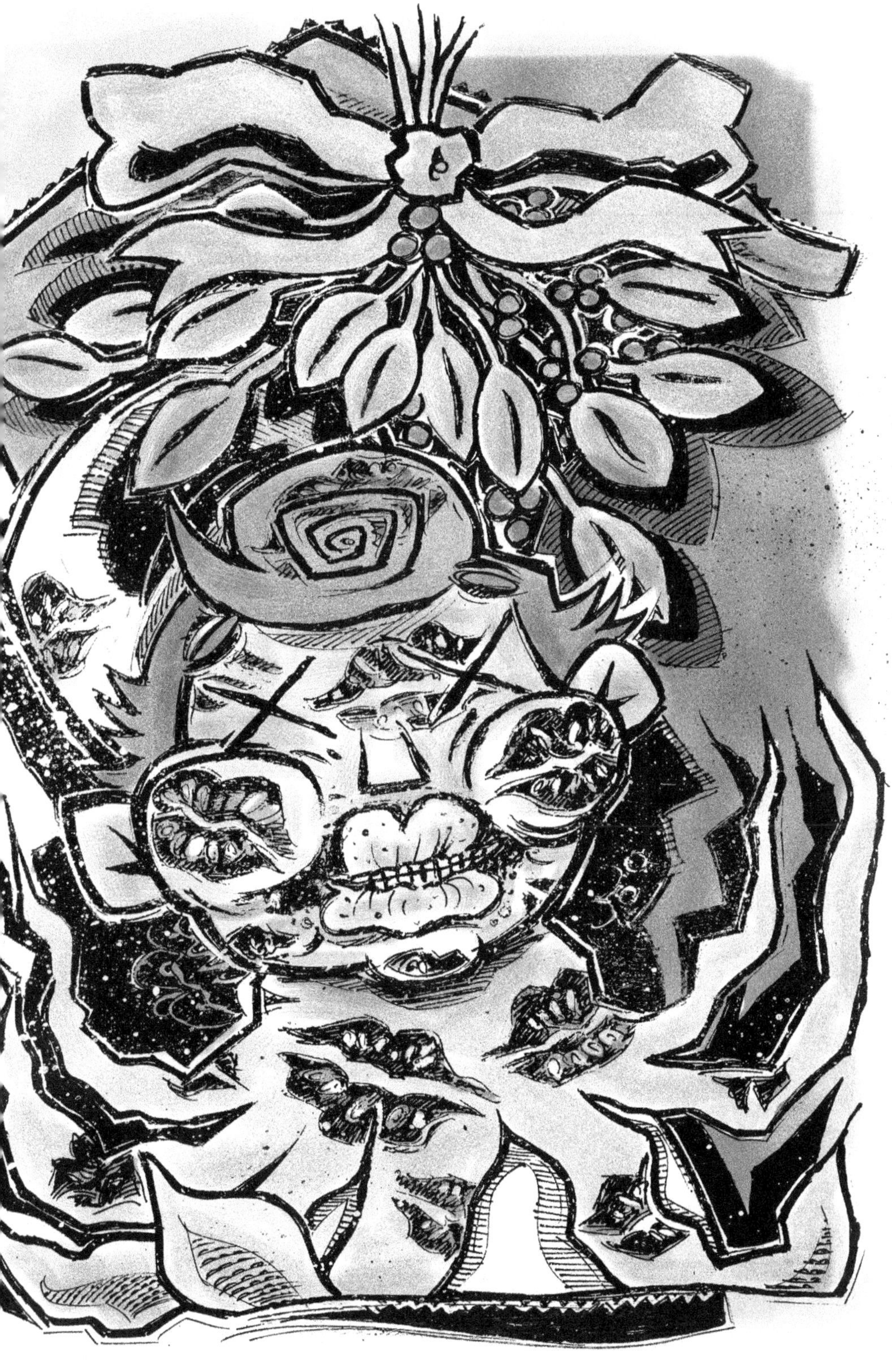

34. NIBBLED TO DEATH BY THE EASTER BUNNY

Don't let its cute smile, pink fur and candy-planting ways fool you: the Easter Bunny is a vicious predator.

Whisper into one of its oversized ears that the entire colony of elves holds nightly feasts of Hasenpfeffer, and the giant rabbit will go to work, making the killer bunny in *Monty Python and the Holy Grail* look like Mahatma Gandhi.

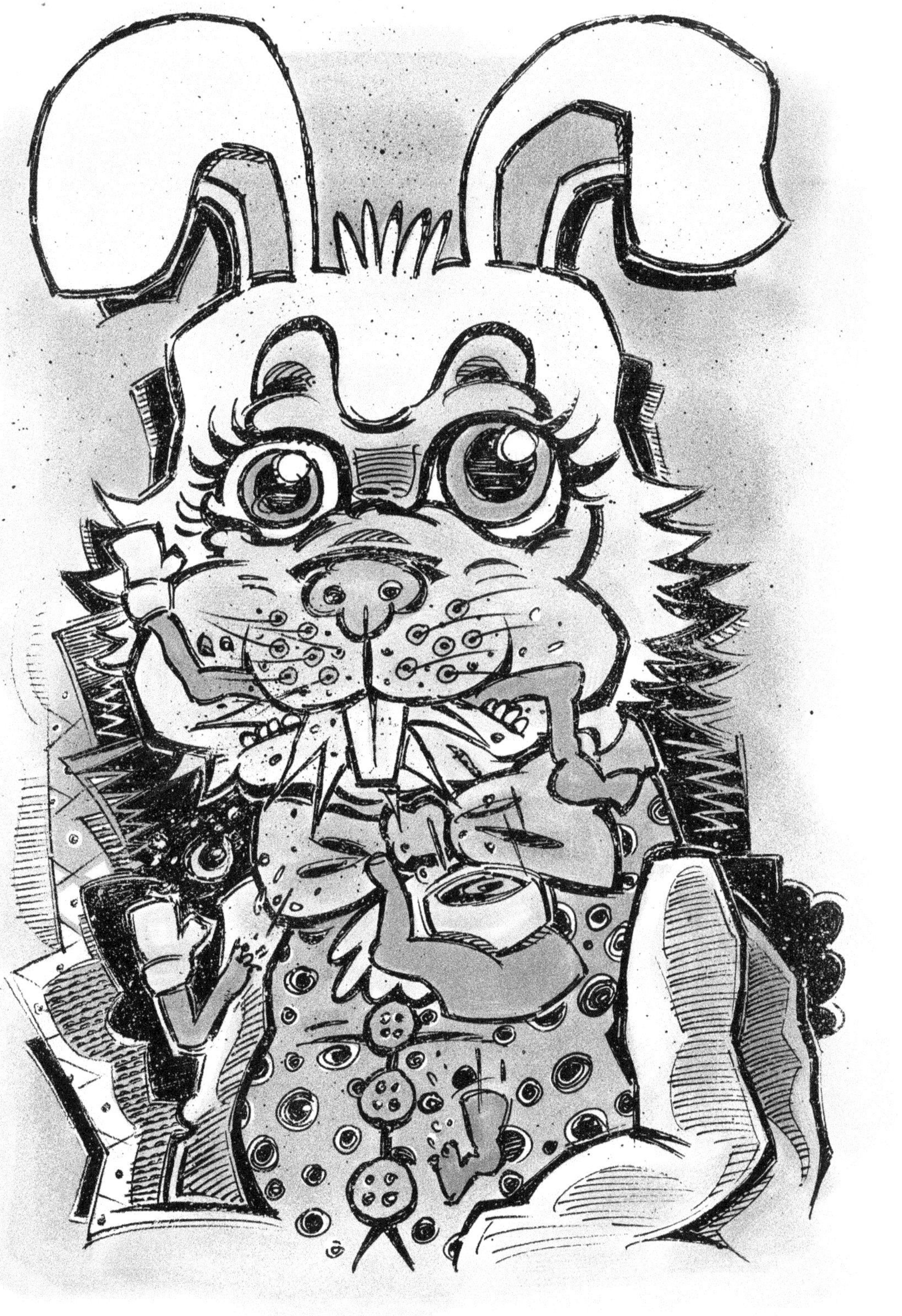

35. INTRODUCE HIM TO THE KRAMPUS

In Alpine winter traditions, Saint Nicholas makes his tour of the villages in the run-up to Christmas with a companion called the Krampus. Both of them carry sacks, but for radically different reasons. While Saint Nick carries gifts in his sack to take care of rewarding the good little boys and girls, the Krampus has a more sinister task: He is in charge of punishing the bad ones. He carries a handful of birch sticks for whipping purposes, and his sack is used as a receptacle for carrying the really bad ones off to Hell.

It wouldn't take much persuasion to convince the Krampus that the elf has been very, very naughty.

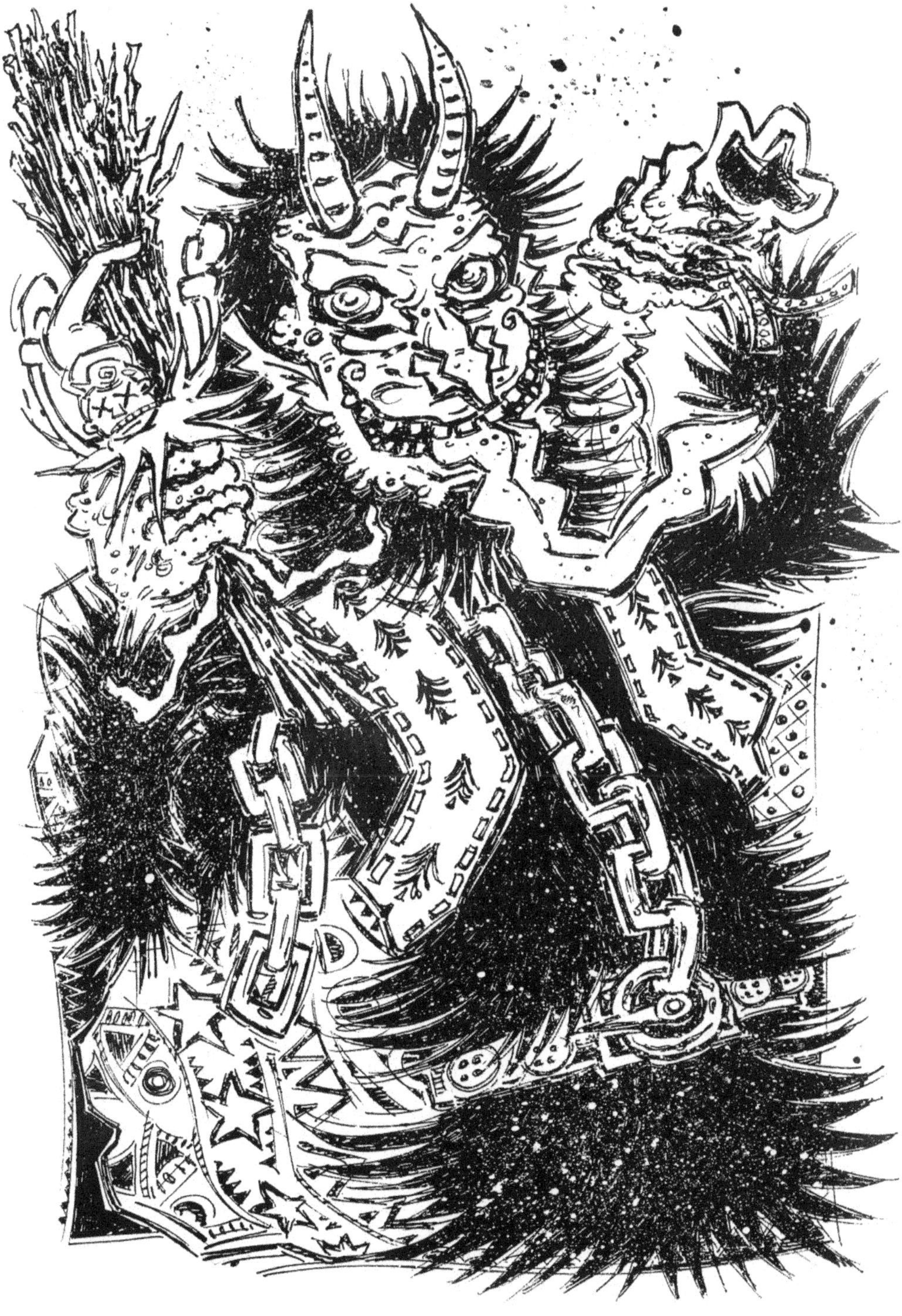

36. USE HIM TO DECORATE YOUR SNOWMAN

Unlike Santa, elves do not carry a whole lot of personal insulation. While Santa weighs as much as three men his size ought to weigh, elves tend to be on the thin side. This means that they are much more prone to hypothermia.

If you ask him to burrow a hole in a snowman's face while you rush off to get a carrot for his nose, you can be sure that by the time you return from the supermarket, your snowman won't need a carrot for his nose.

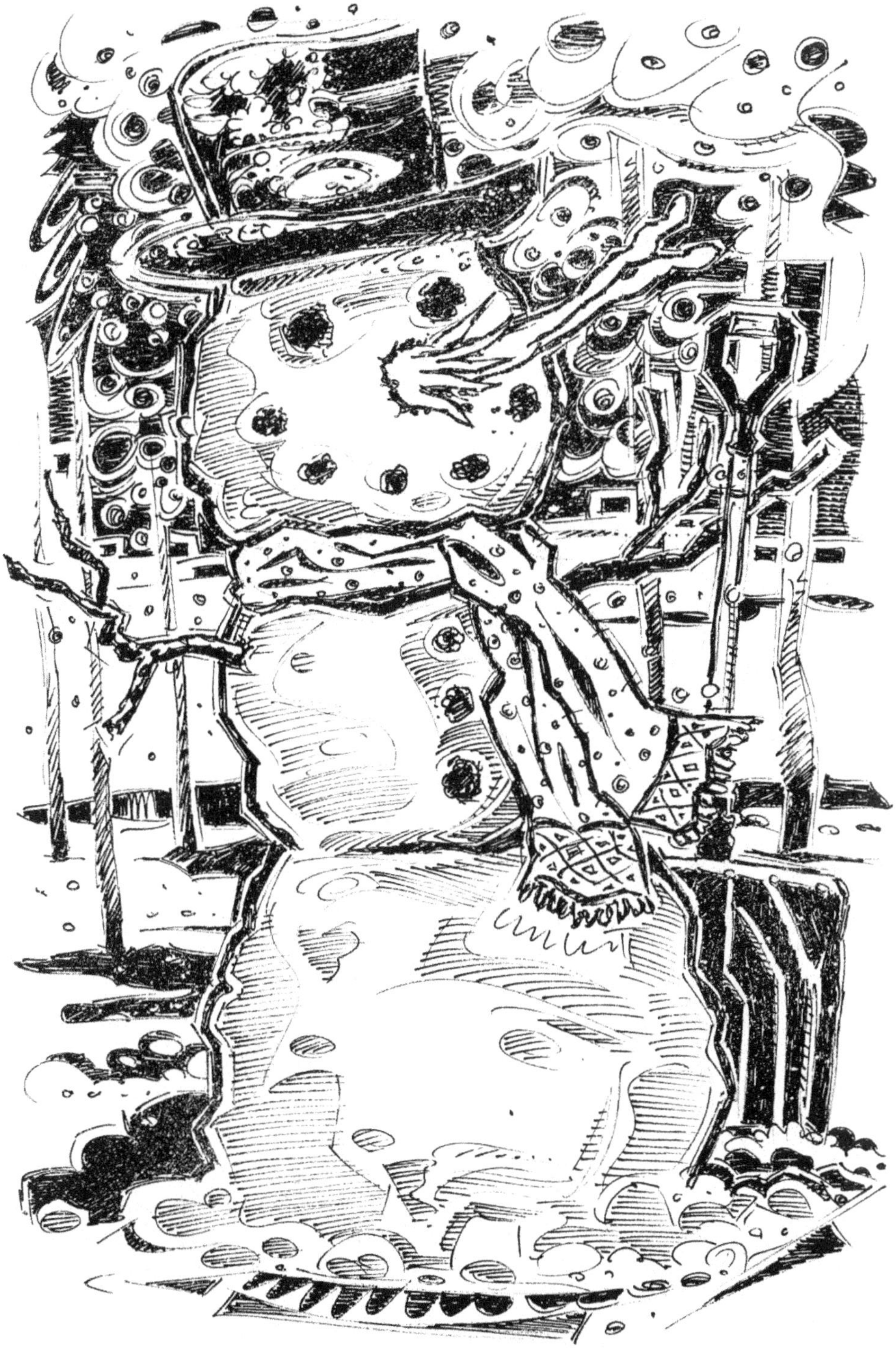

37. CLEAR HIM AND THE SNOW FROM THE PAVEMENT

After the next heavy snowfall, ask your elf to help with clearing the walkways around your house. Hand him a little shovel and promise him a warm mug of hot chocolate when he's done. And advise him to wear thick earmuffs so his little ears won't get cold.

When he gets started, call out to him a few times to see whether sound is penetrating the earmuffs. If he doesn't respond, fire up the snowblower...

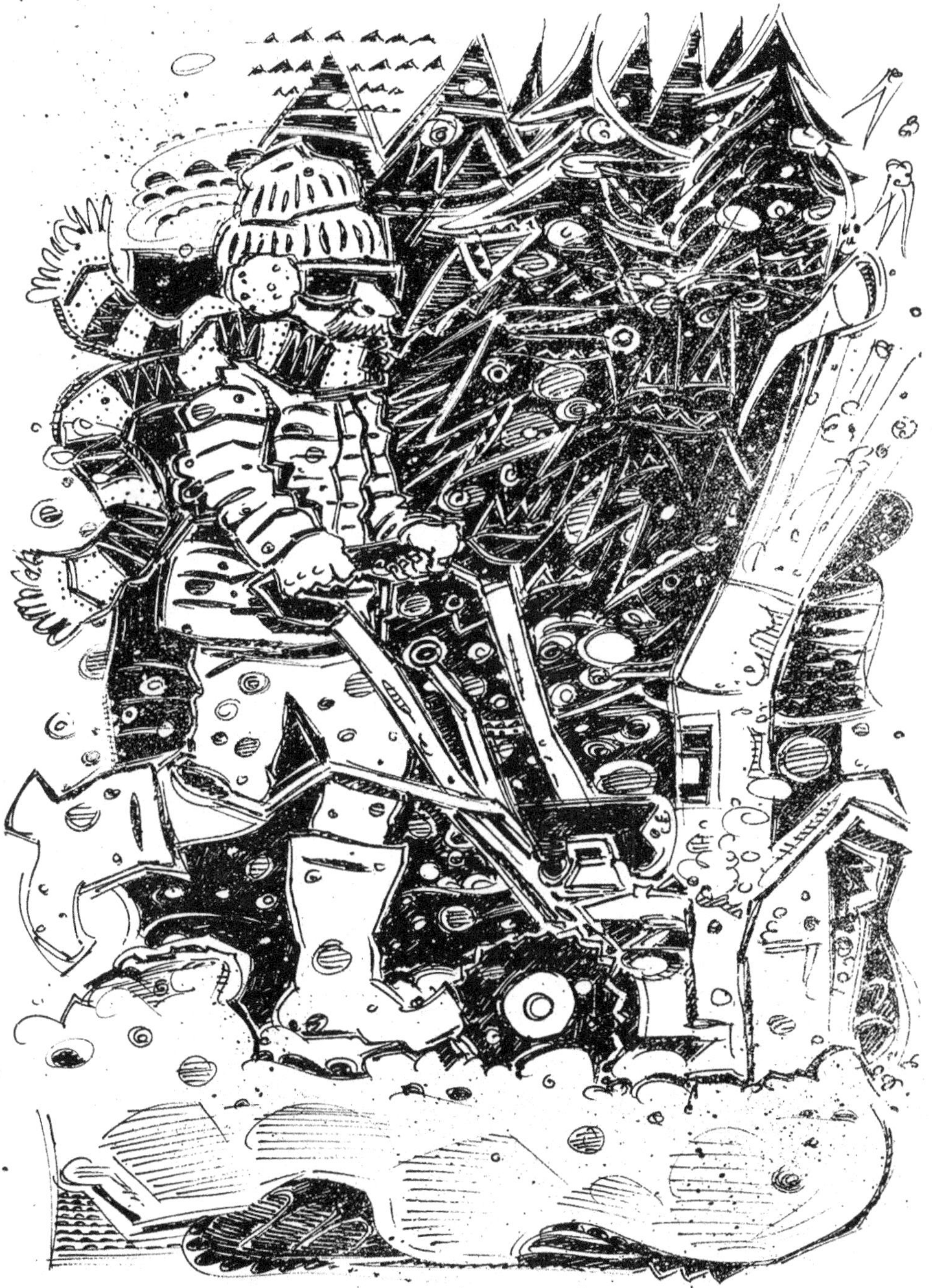

38. FLUSH HIM WITH SUCCESS

Elves are among us to spy on children and report back to the NSA (NorthPole Security Administration). The elf's propensity for nosiness is among its biggest weaknesses.

First, spray cooking oil over the seat and bowl of your toilet. Inform your elf victim that something naughty is going on in the bathroom, possibly the old plastic-wrap-under-the-toilet-seat trick. When the elf goes to inspect the plumbing, he will slip into the water, and the lubricated porcelain will be impossible for him to climb out again.

When you hear splashing and squeaky cries for help, enter the room and flush repeatedly until all traces are gone. This technique is especially gratifying on airplanes.

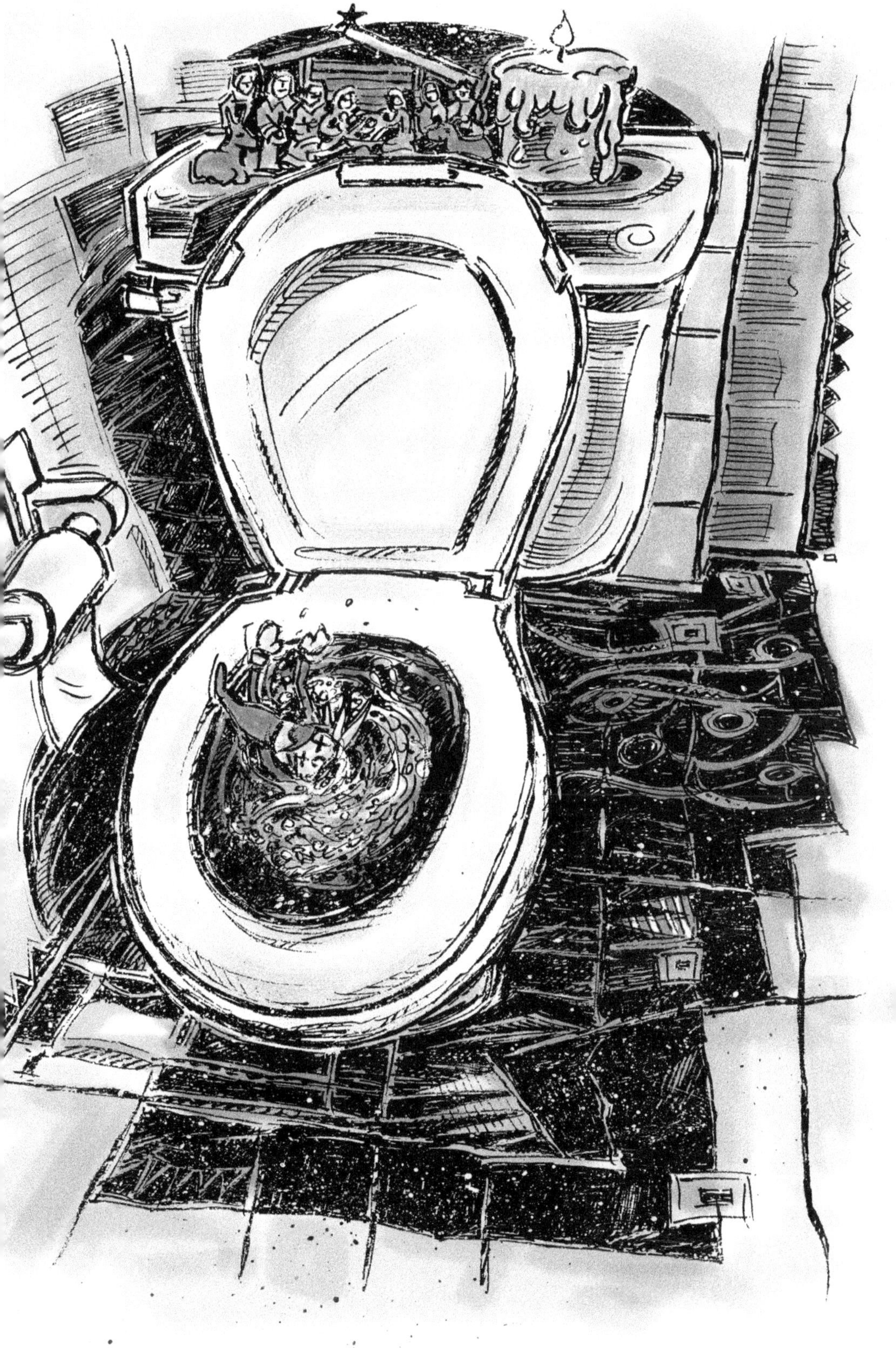

39. ONE WORD: NUTCRACKER

Send an anonymous tip to Herr Drosselmeyer that the elf is a double agent: Not only does he spy for Santa Claus, he also feeds intelligence to the mouse army.

If that fails, spread word among the gingerbread men that the elf made lewd comments during the Dance of the Sugar Plum Fairy.

The Nutcracker will take care of the rest.

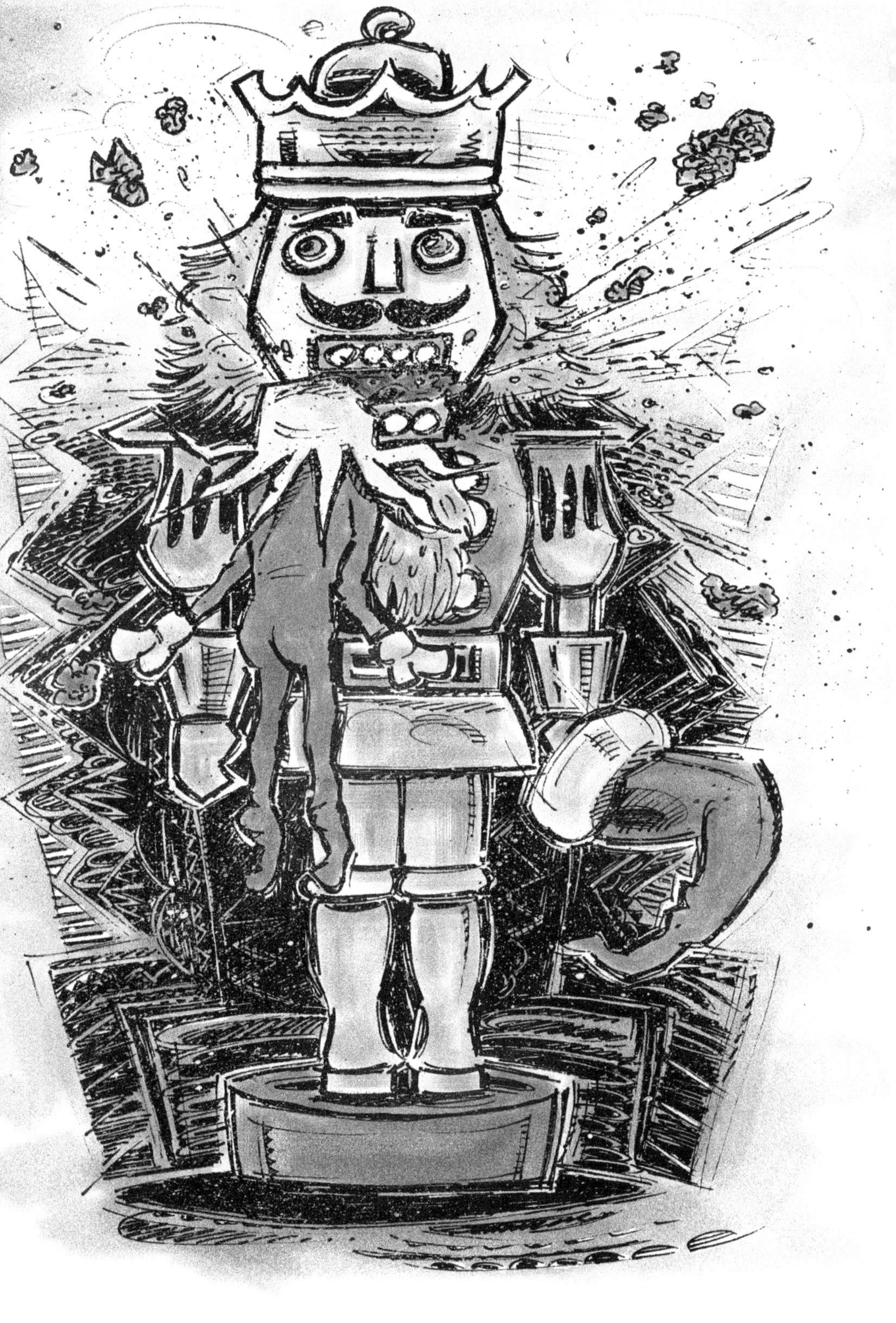

40. SAT ON BY A MALL SANTA

This technique is all about timing and playing with the natural vanity of the elf species. You can tell from the coy look on their apple-cheeked faces that elves just love themselves. So persuading an elf to pose for a photograph will pose no problems. Timing it so that Santa is on a five-minute break when you arrive at Santa's Mall Grotto takes more skill.

Tell your elf that you really want to take a picture of him on Santa's chair. Slip past Mall Santa's helpers. Install the elf on the chair and take lots of photographs. When Santa shows up, distract the big guy just enough that he doesn't look down before he sits.

With all the padding he carries on his hindquarters, Santa won't even feel the elfin death throes beneath him.

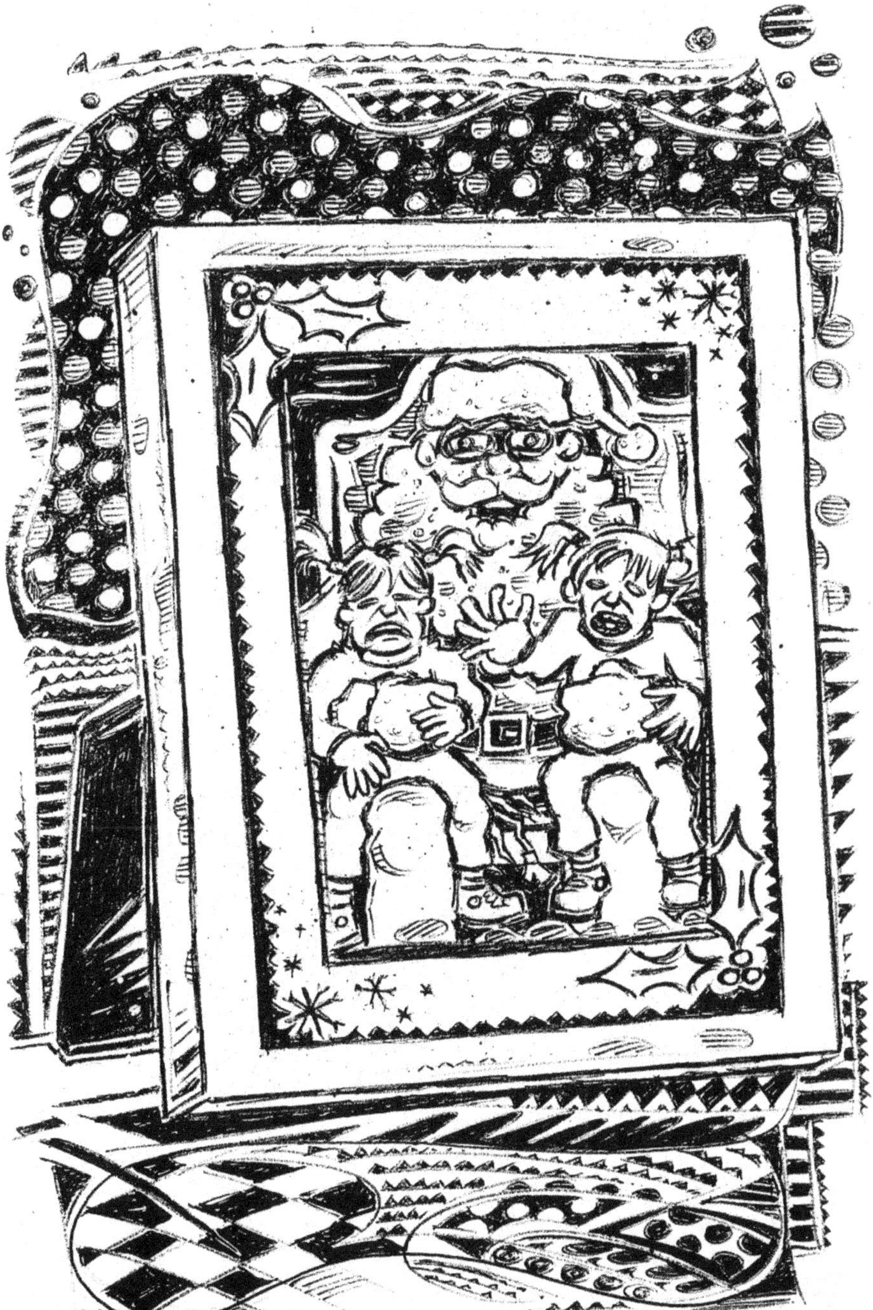

41. TIED TO THE TRACKS OF THE POLAR EXPRESS

In 1985, Chris Van Allsburg composed and illustrated a wonderful book about a kid in his PJ's taking a train to the North Pole to see Santa. In 2004, Warner Bros Pictures adapted a CGI animated adaptation of story into an uncanny valley that not even Tom Hanks's voice could soften. The Polar Express has since mutated into a real train.

Across the United States, Canada, and Great Britain, no fewer than 45 trains are branded as the Polar Express, and offered up as official holiday rides. This gives elf exterminators a great opportunity. Remember: Elves are not the sharpest tools on the shelf. Tell your intended victim that everyone takes naps on train tracks.

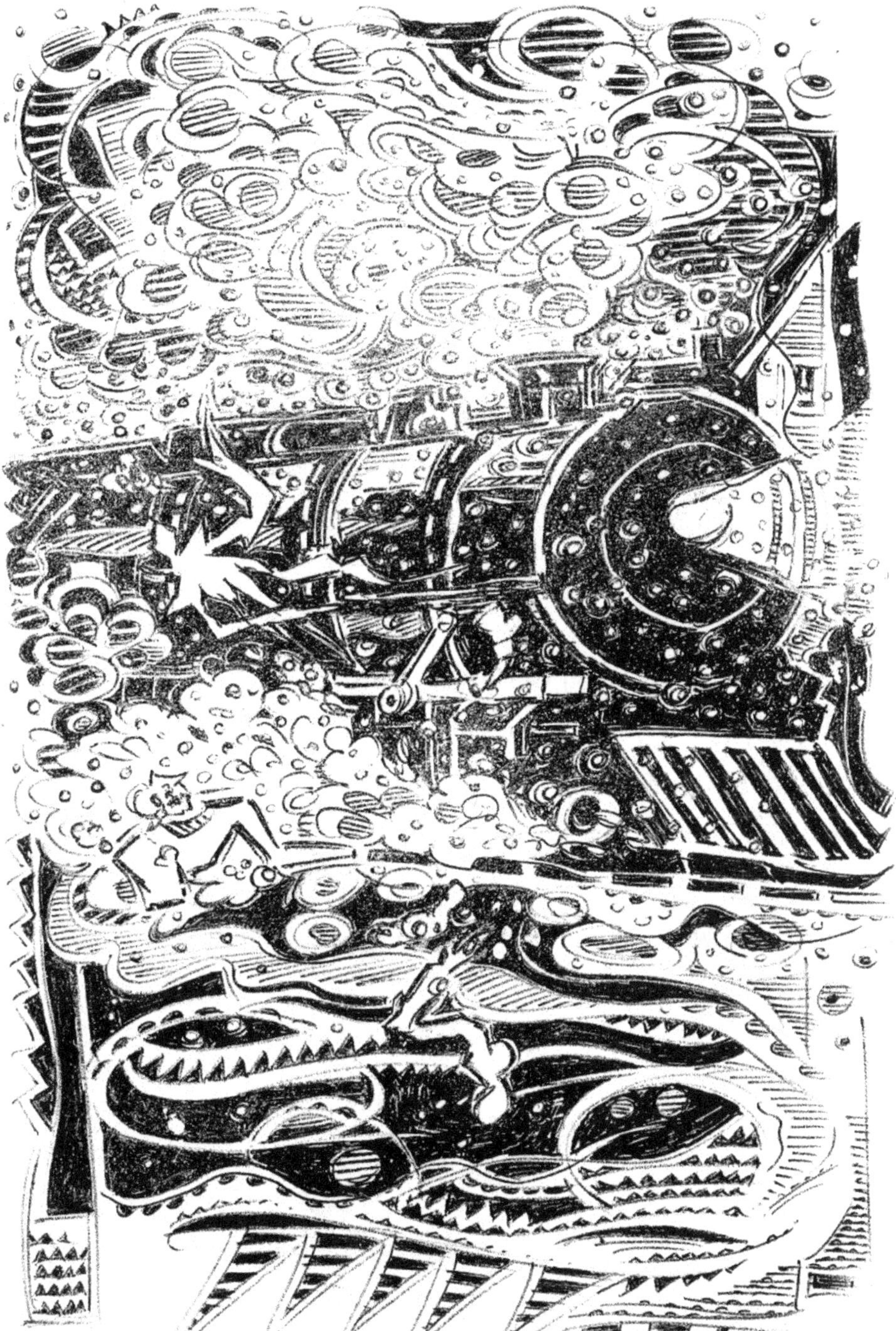

42. DRESS HIM IN CATNIP PAJAMAS

For families with particularly large and grumpy cats, there is no better way to control a rampant elf population problem than to use the dangerous relaxing habits of the feline members of the household.

Leave out festively wrapped clothing with a gift tag caption of "To A Dear Elf." See to it that the clothing is infused with the feline neurostimulator catnip, which inevitably drives the feline species into a frenzy of sitting down on anything that smells of it.

The elf will wear the clothing. The cat will sit on him. The deed will be done.

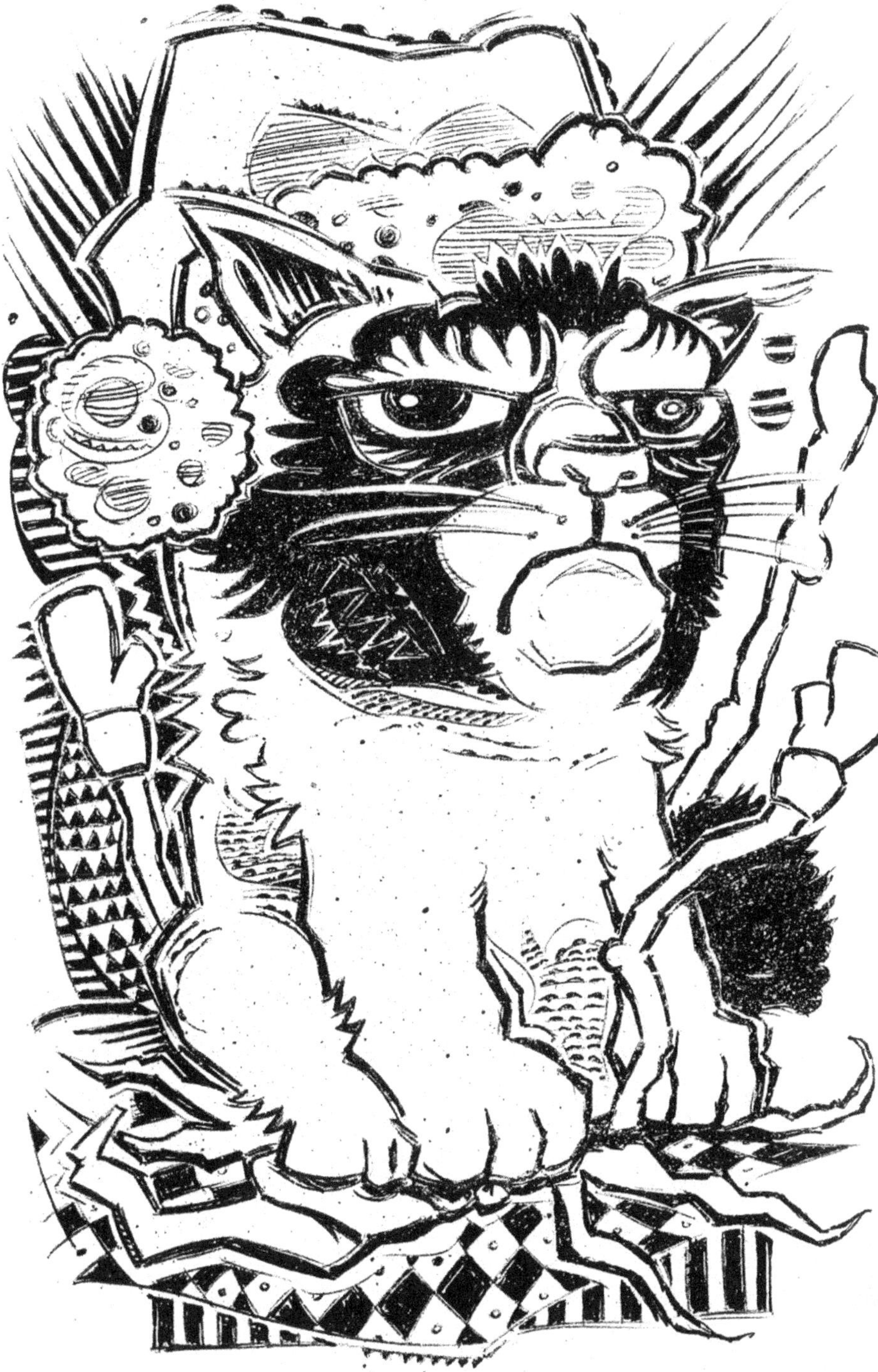

43. SUPERCHARGE HIS CHRISTMAS CRACKER

In the 1840s, right around the time Charles Dickens unleashed his tale of Ebenezer Scrooge on the world, another Londoner was experimenting with different kind of tradition for the holidays. His name was Tom Smith, inventor of an explosive novelty to boost the revenues of his ailing candy business. He called it the Christmas cracker, a festively decorated tube containing a paper crown and novelties and a tiny pinch of gunpowder that let out a small explosion when you pulled the cracker at each end.

Christmas crackers endure to this day, and with a minor modification they can be used to control the elf population. Instead of using the traditional paper crown and novelty, you stuff the cracker at both ends with volatile explosives such as Semtex or nitroglycerine. Hand the cracker to two elves and bid them a Merry Christmas, while making a hasty retreat to safety.

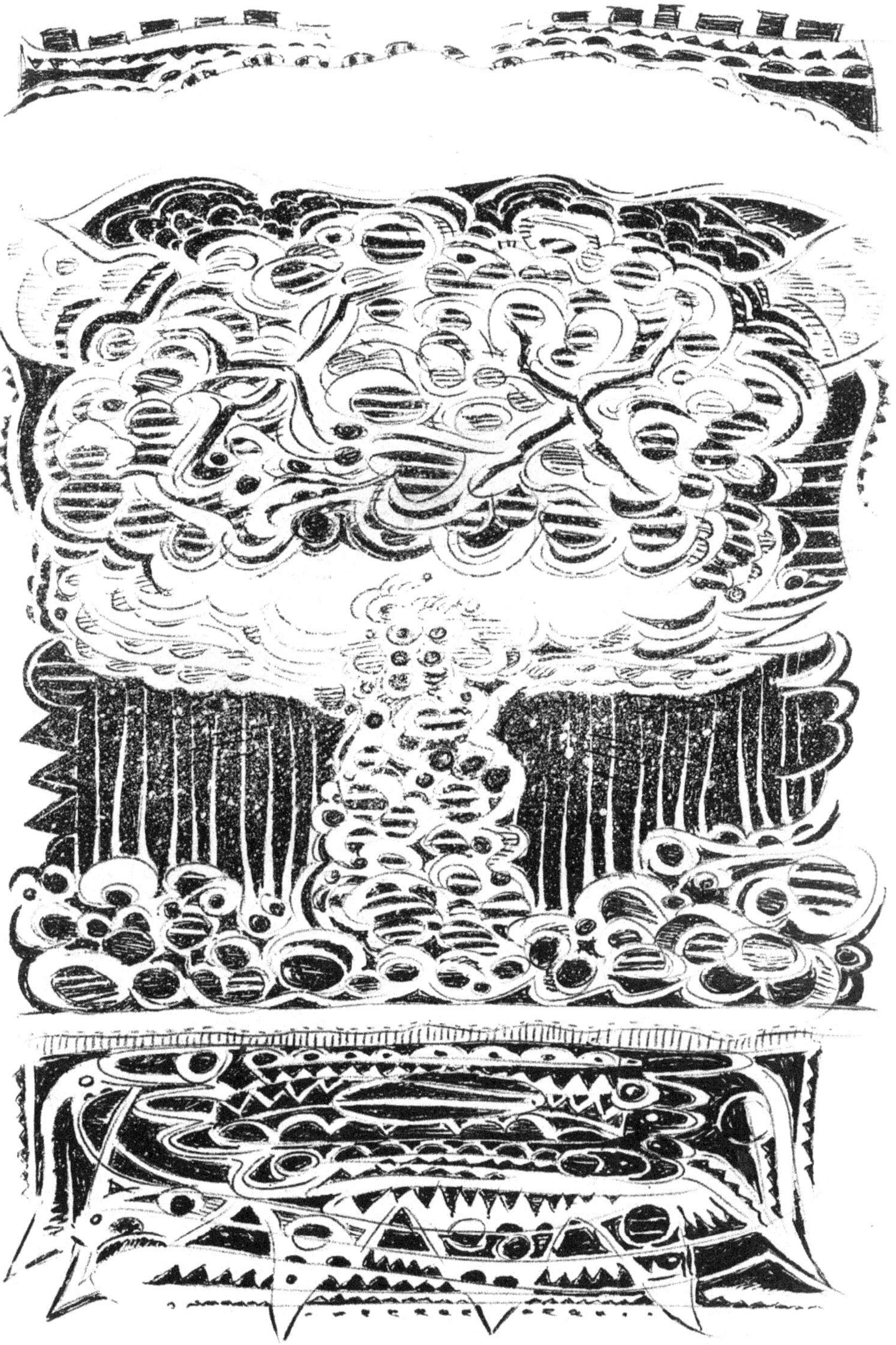

44. MAROONED ON THE ISLAND OF MISFIT TOYS

The horrors that await an elf on the Island of Misfit Toys are too terrible to elaborate upon. The animated version you have seen on a certain CBS holiday special bears little resemblance to the real thing. The true dangers lurking there were censored to protect the fragile structure of your sanity from thoughts that would shatter your peace of mind forever.

The real counterparts of those characters—the winged lion King Moonracer, the terrifyingly misnamed Charlie-In-The-Box, the polka dotted elephant, swimming bird, and ostrich-riding cowboy—exude the same aura of menace that Alfred Hitchcock was shooting for in The Birds and Psycho.

Do not, under any circumstances, go to the Island of Misfit Toys yourself. Just buy a one-way ticket there for your elf, and try not to think too hard about what will happen to him there.

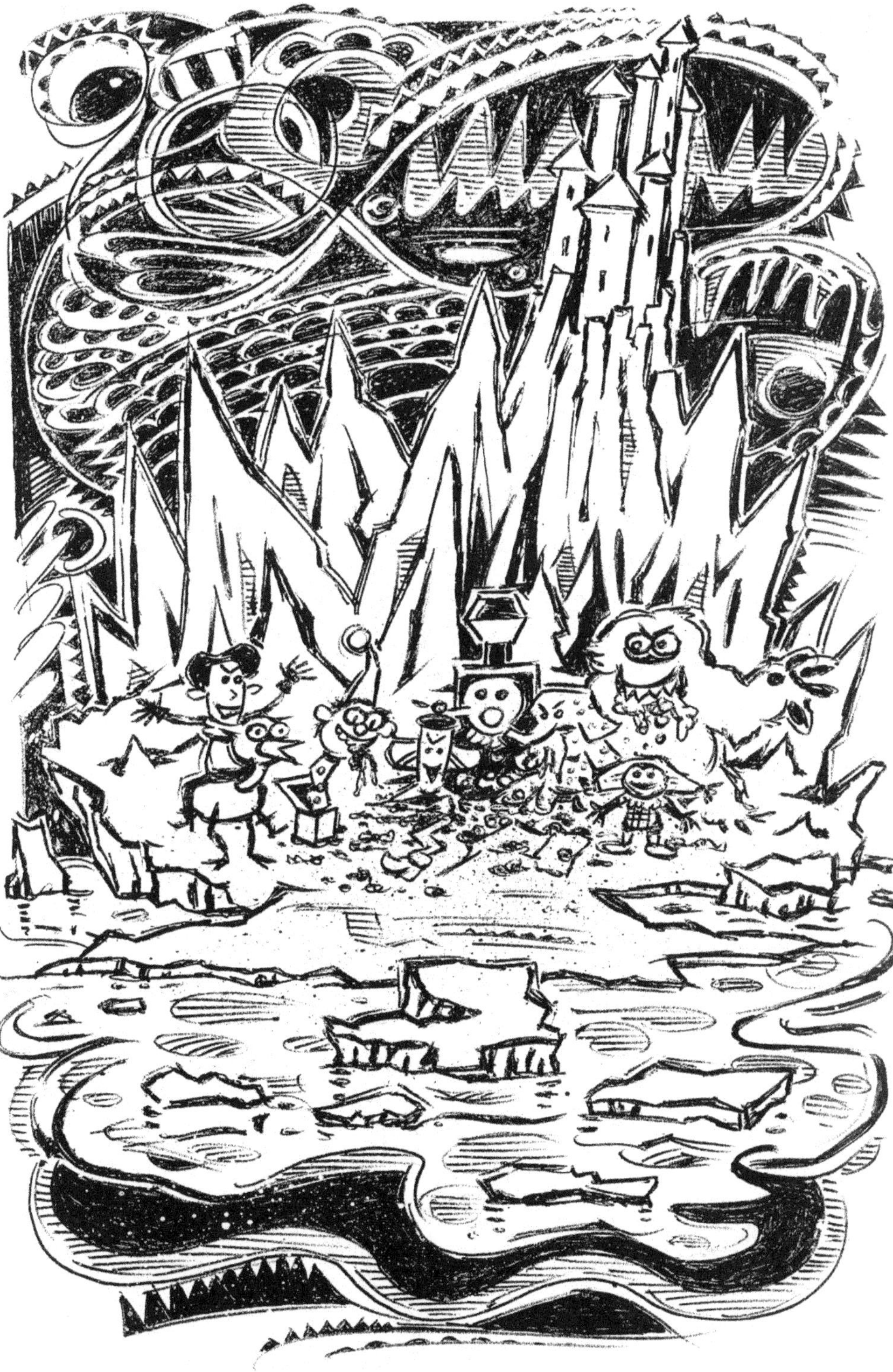

45. MUGGED BY A GINGER WITH A CANDY CANE

Redheads make up a tiny proportion of the world's population. Only two people in a hundred have hair that is naturally at the end of the spectrum occupied by russet and auburn tones.

You can call these fiery individuals many things with impunity: Celt, firebrand, red-head, Weasley. But you cannot call them after that spice you make little cookie men out of. Many of them actively hate being called that; it causes them to erupt in a furious conflagration. Coincidentally, the gingerbread men share the same trigger.

Convince an elf that gingerbread men like being called "ginge" or "gingey." Introduce him to one, then wait for the delicious little guy to take care of the rest.

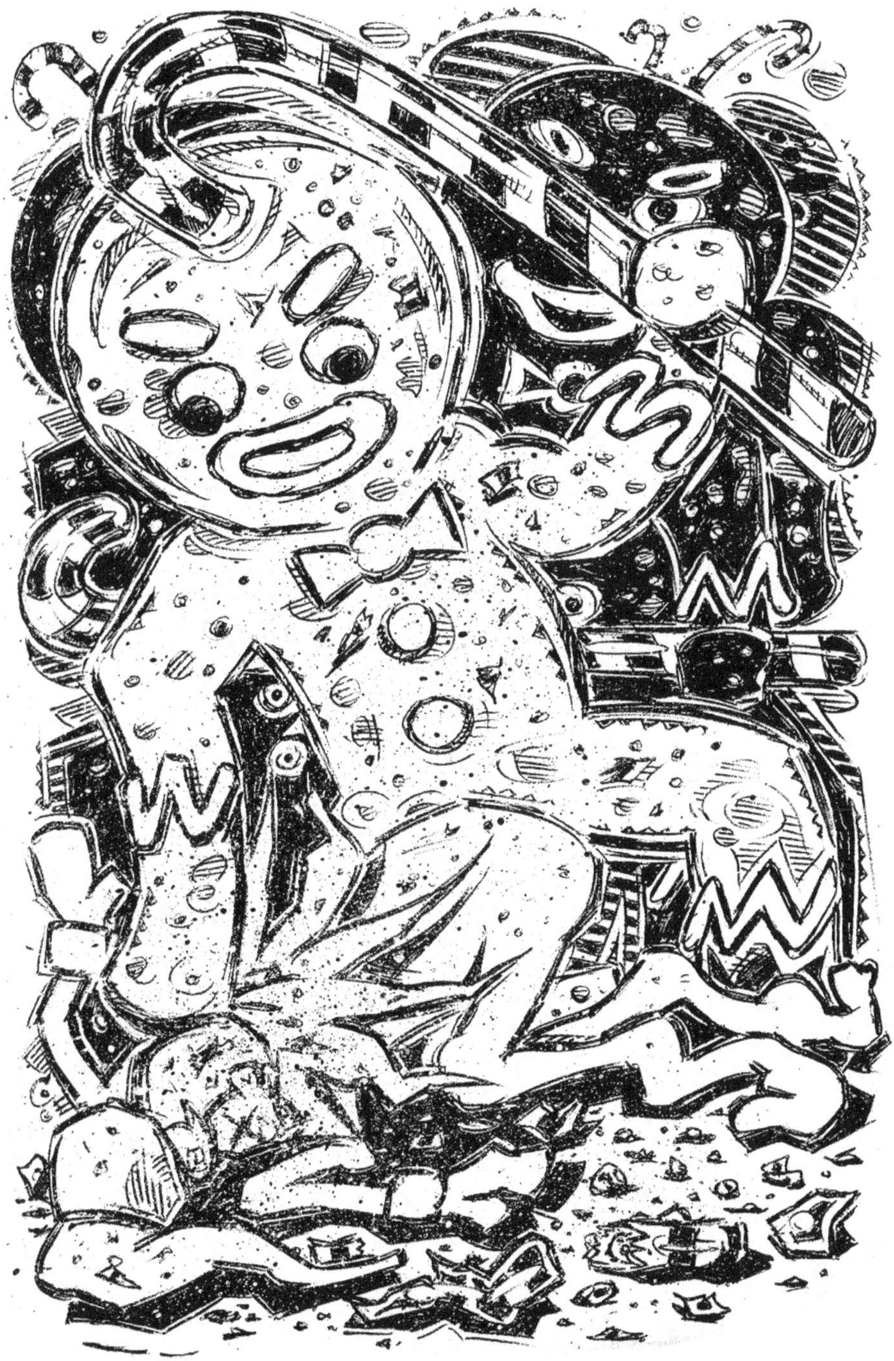

46. TAKE HIM TO SEE THE MANNHEIM STEAMROLLER

It has been argued that no single musical group in history has been as closely associated with any festival holiday as Mannheim Steamroller is with Christmas. Since 1984, the Omaha-native band released more than twenty albums of Christmas music...and precious little else.

Elves envy anything with a greater association to Christmas than themselves. They crave the warm glow of Christmasness that washes over everyone in the thrall of Mannheim Steamroller. So it won't be hard to entrap your elf with the promise of a special meet-and-greet session with the band.

Except that when the elf gets there, the encounter will be with a regular non-Mannheim type of steamroller. This type of substitution is perfectly legal as long as you print a disclaimer on the special meet-and-greet ticket stating that the offer is subject to the availability of the band, and that other steamrollers may be substituted in the event that the band cannot be present at the appointed time.

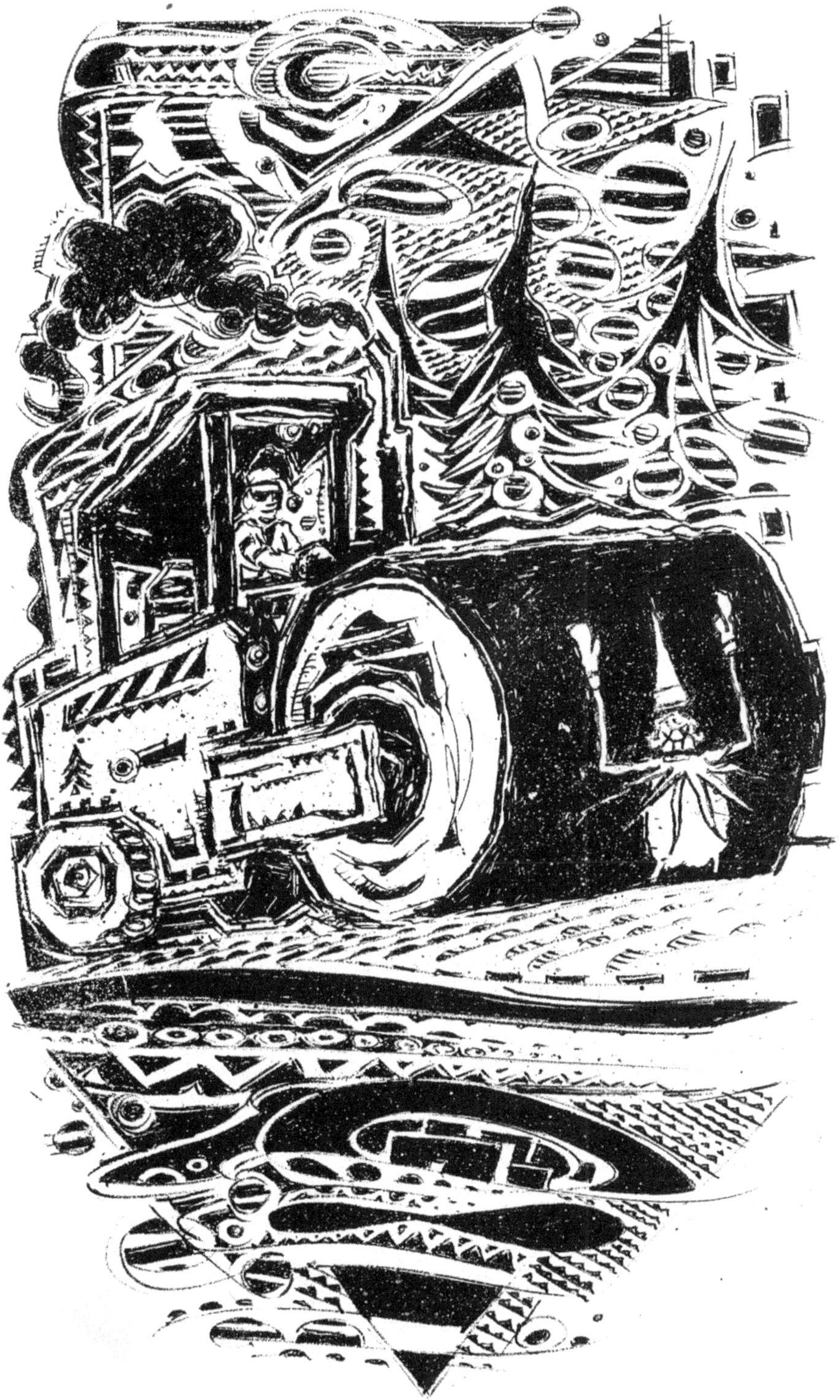

47. CURIOSITY KILLED THE ELF

Young children are not only are they short of stature, but also of patience. It is a torture to them to have Christmas presents under the tree that they cannot unwrap. Use this trait in your quest to control the elf population.

While your elf is asleep, gently move his little elf mattress into a box with sharp blades protruding, iron maiden-style, from five sides. Decorate the outside of the box with festive wrapping paper, bows, ribbons, and a name tag addressed to that most inquisitive child of the house.

Wait for curiosity to take hold.

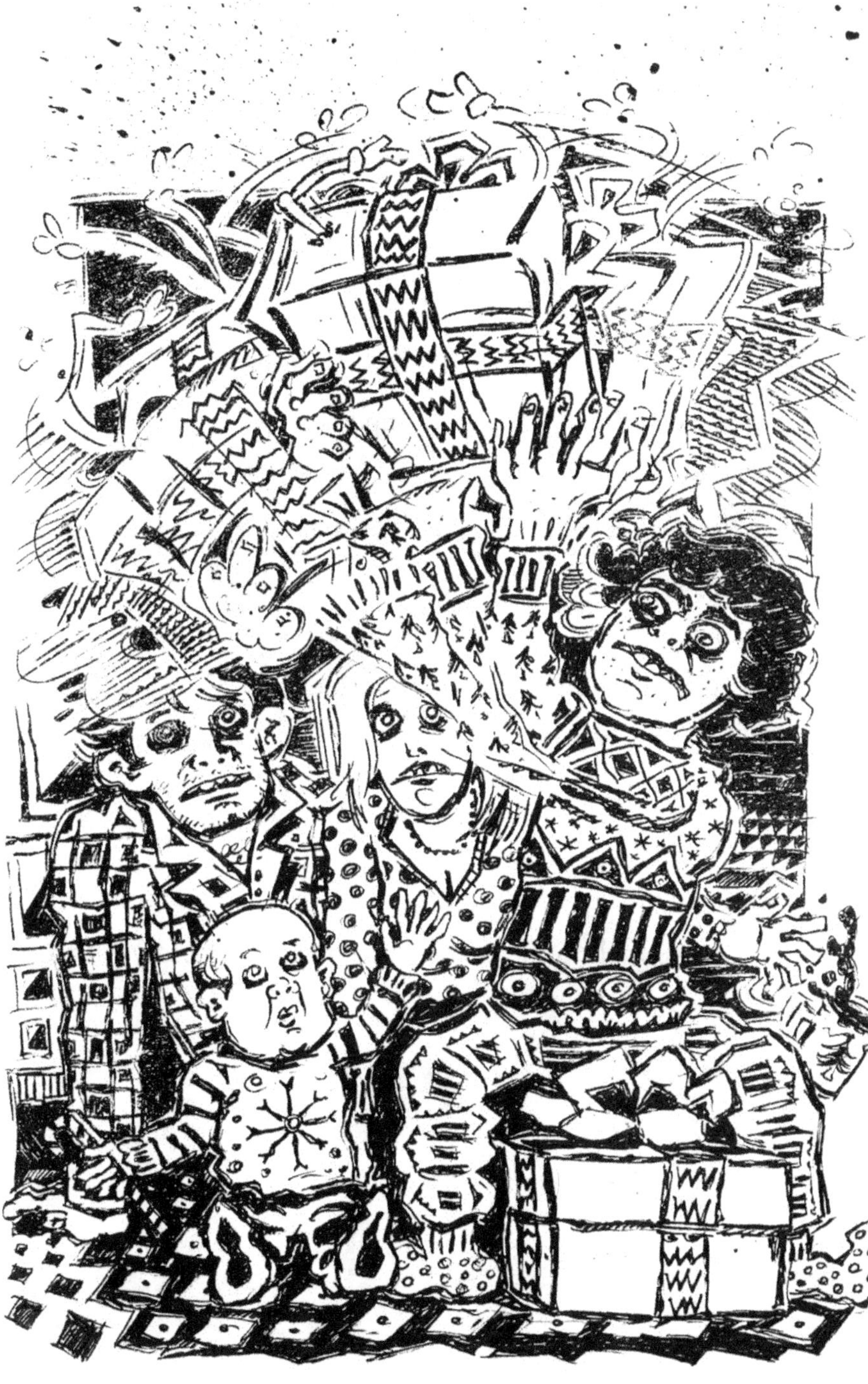

48. CONFUCIUS SAY: PUT ELF IN FORTUNE COOKIE

Imagine the poor family in A Christmas Story at Christmas lunchtime: They have already opened their Zeppelins, Red Ryder B.B. Guns, and bowling balls. The Bumpus's dogs have made off with their turkey. There has been much weeping. And they go off to the local Chinese restaurant looking for solace.

Now imagine how happy that family would be to open their fortune cookies and see an elf folded up inside. Imagine the smiles. Imagine the plummy narration of some Jean Shepherd monologue describing it all.

All you need to do is figure out how to make this happen. May we suggest mailing your elf to the nearest fortune cookie factory with a polite letter?

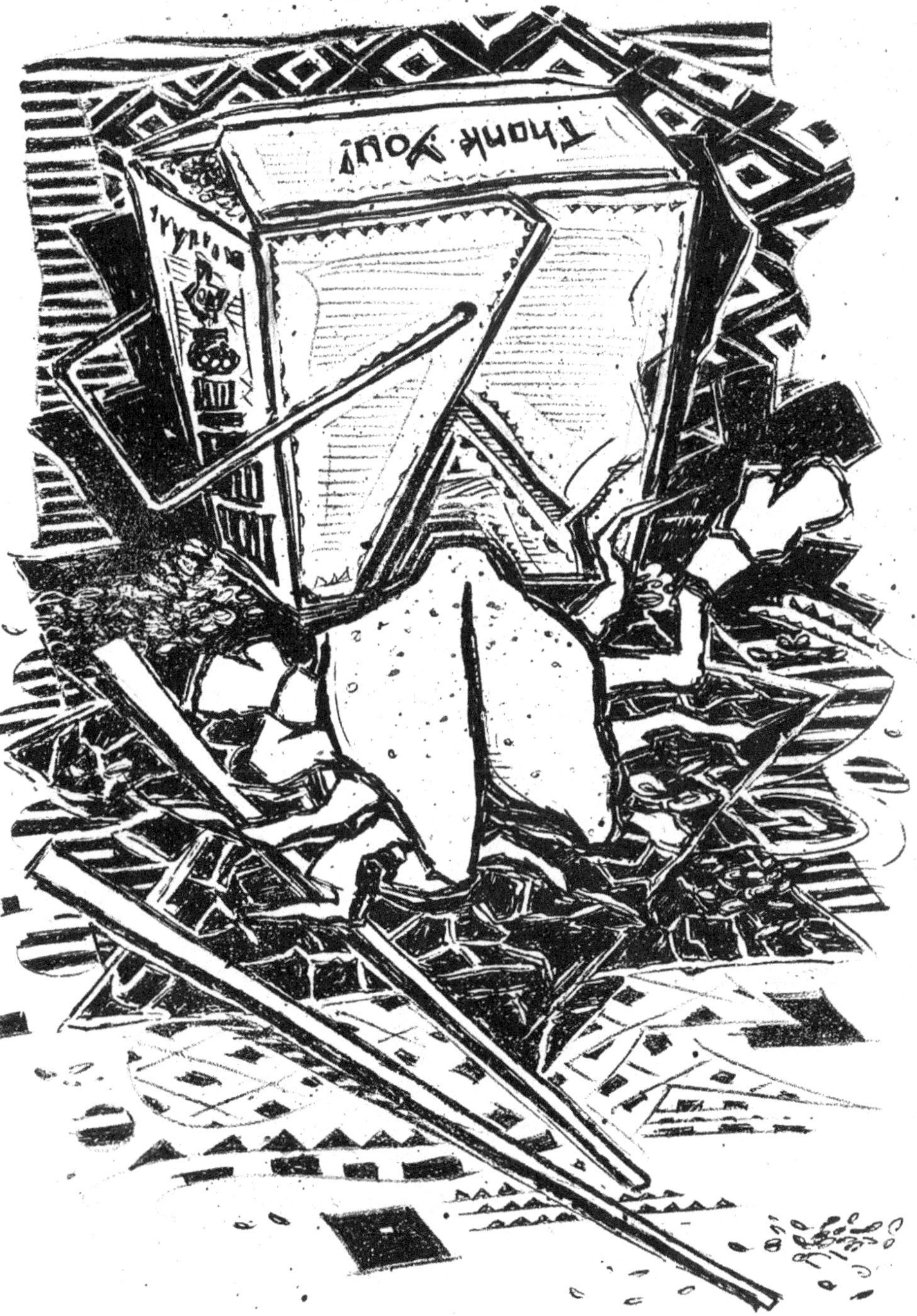
Thank You!

49. THE BLACK FRIDAY MASSACRE

Here's a fun fact: You are statistically more likely to die at a retail outlet on the day after Thanksgiving (0.87 average annual deaths) than you are from running from a bovine stampede during Pamplona's Running of the Bulls festival (0.13).

On the last Friday of this November, just ask an elf to hold your place in the line for the $98 big-screen TVs. Then beat a hasty retreat to the security camera room and watch the law of averages take care of the rest.

Alternatively, ask him to sit in your shopping trolley. Before you fill it with bargains.

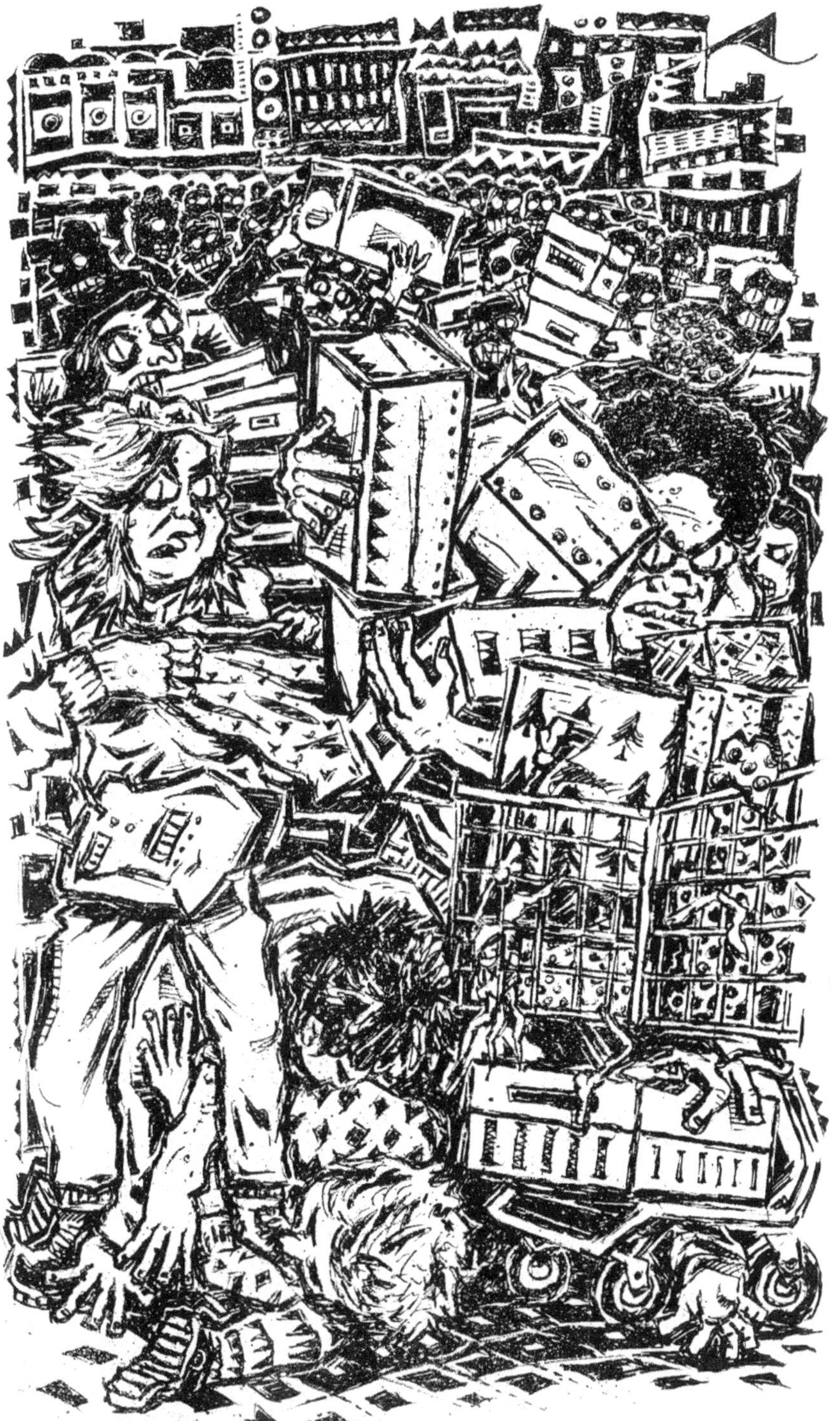

50. JUST LEAVE HIM ON THE SHELF

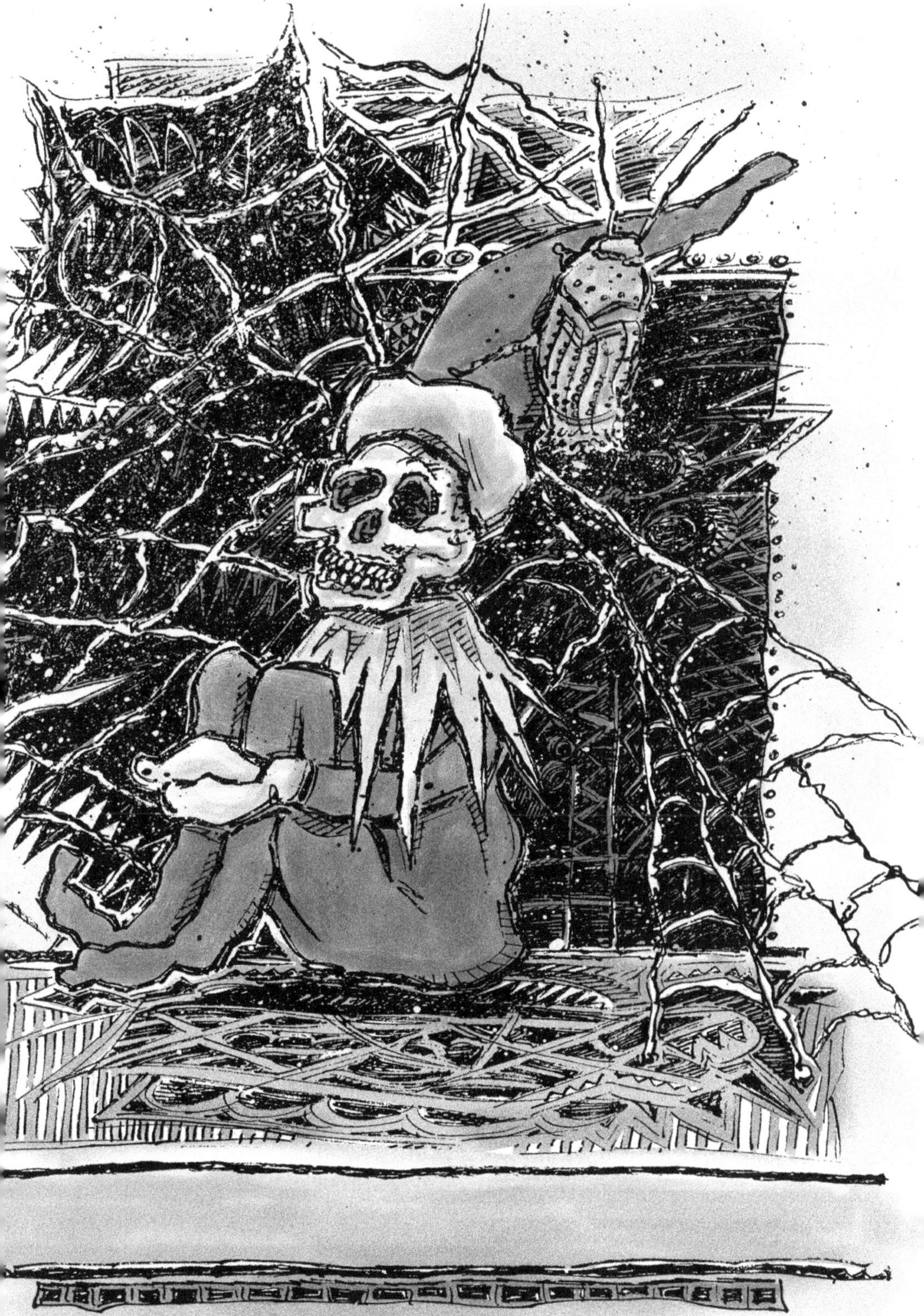

ABOUT THE AUTHORS

James Lincke and Matt Lake really hate elves.

I mean, really really hate elves.

IF YOU HATED THIS BOOK,
YOU'LL ABSOLUTELY LOATHE

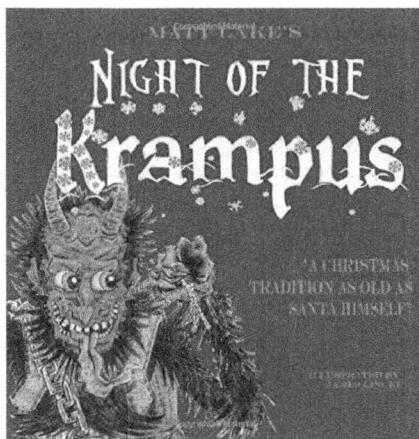

NIGHT OF THE
Krampus

Night of the Krampus by Matt Lake and James Lincke

ISBN-10: 0692495223   ISBN-13: 978-0692495223

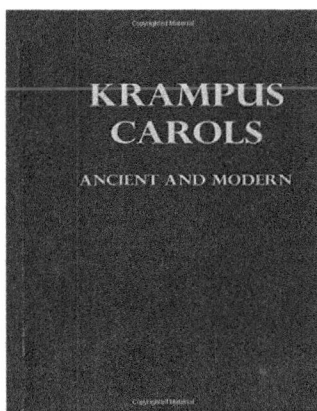

KRAMPUS
CAROLS
ANCIENT AND MODERN

Krampus Carols Ancient And Modern by Matt Lake

ISBN-10: 151775982X ISBN-13: 978-1517759827

www.ingramcontent.com/pod-product-compliance
Lightning Source LLC
Chambersburg PA
CBHW060122050426
42448CB00010B/2002
* 9 7 8 0 6 9 2 5 8 9 9 7 7 *